M000033888

Ode to the Cold War

▼

ODE TO THE COLD WAR
POEMS NEW AND SELECTED

Dick Allen

Sarabande Books
LOUISVILLE, KENTUCKY

Copyright © 1971, 1975, 1984, 1987, 1997 by Dick Allen
FIRST EDITION
All rights reserved.

No part of this book may be reproduced without written
permission of the publisher. Please direct inquiries to:

Managing Editor
Sarabande Books, Inc.
2234 Dundee Road, Suite 200
Louisville, KY 40205

ISBN: 0-9641151-9-0 Cloth
        1-889330-00-0 Paper

Library of Congress Cataloging-in-Publication Data

Allen, Dick, 1939–
    Ode to the Cold War : poems new & selected / by Dick Allen. — 1st ed.
        p.   cm.
    ISBN 0-9641151-9-0 (cloth : acid-free paper). — ISBN 1-889330-00-0
(pbk. : acid-free paper)
    I. Title.
PS3551.L3922033   1997
811'.54—dc20   96-25051
                                                              CIP

Cover Painting: *April Wind* by Andrew Newell Wyeth.
Wadsworth Atheneum, Hartford. Gift of Mr. and Mrs. Joseph R. Swan.
Reproduced by kind permission.

Cover and text design by Charles Casey Martin.

Manufactured in the United States of America.
This book is printed on acid-free paper.

Sarabande Books is a nonprofit literary organization.

To Lori
forever and ever
▼

Contents

▼

from OVERNIGHT IN THE GUEST HOUSE OF THE MYSTIC (1984)

from FLIGHT AND PURSUIT (1987)

Ode to the Cold War

▼

New Poems

(1997)

TIME TO HEAR OURSELVES THINK

We've missed that for years, not so much
The thinking itself—that goes on regardless—
But the hearing of it, small waterwheels
Turning in millponds, the press and hiss

Of steam irons in storefront laundry shops,
Gears changing, the tick in the clock
Hopping upstairs. It's as if,
In muffled slow motion, through shock and aftershock,

We kept feeling with our hands—all thought
Outside ourselves, all concepts
Those railroad stations we were always leaving,
Elevators, the courthouse steps

Hurrying toward collapse. But now that we have
Stolen this time, I'm beginning
To hear numbers—I swear it—
Little formations of numbers gathering

Strength as their flanks swing east, and pigeons
Cooing in bank alcoves, and my own
Pencil tapping, ears popping, the spitting sound
Made when tires roll over tiny stones

And it's almost frightening to think
Of what was going on, how much lies there
Scattered, or wounded, or dead
In ourselves that we could not hear.

BLANKET WEATHER

Down from the attic they come, the old thick blankets
In our family for years: two Thomas Early's,
A Hudson's Bay Point, a Chief Joseph,
And the barracks-green army ones our fathers slept beneath
At Hanover Field, and Bastogne. We put up the storms,
Caulk, and rake curlers of maple leaves against the house,
Comfortable in our sweaters. At lakeshore
Our neighbors pull their rowboats from the water,
Turn them over, covering them in tarps
Held down with large stones. A Connecticut chimney sweeper
Waves his top hat from a nearby roof,
And although it's too early for snow, each evening
The sky has seemed heavier, whiter,
Wind shifting to the north. Streetlights go on
Just after supper, gathering knots of boys and girls,
Skateboards and bikes. There's something Eakins about it:
The colors, the calm, the pleasurable sense in waiting
For so much out of our hands. We begin
Imagining frost birds coming to our windows,
Radiator steam, slippers beneath the bed
As we unfold the blankets, shake them out between us,
One with the almost-not-there mothball smell
That reminds you of oaken chests, stored wedding gowns,
Their lace browning slowly as the backs of elderly hands,
And the Armed Services Editions
Of *The Razor's Edge, The Citadel, The Daniel Jazz*
That lay deep in rafters beside the huge glass eyes and snout
Of a gas mask your father carried as he walked beside the tanks,
Toward the war's end. Is it too sentimental
To say we now are living what they once fought for
Approaching fifty years ago? I've ordered a cord
Of fireplace wood to be delivered to the shed,
Changed the antifreeze, and switched to a heavier jacket
On my nightly strolls through the suburbs

To the end of Robinwood Lane, where I bend
Onto Booth Hill until it reaches Fern Circle
And the peaceful houses set back from their dormant lawns.
I shiver, blow on my fingers, looking forward
To crawling beneath the blankets and the slight
Scratch of wool as I turn to your warming body
Under the striped patterns, the indigo lines,
A small boat drifting from a jeering crew,
The Nez Perce of Wallowa Valley, laying down their weapons
Forty miles from Canada—and December,
1944: the battle for our lives.

LETTER FROM A
CONNECTICUT COUNTRY HOUSE

I

The fuchsia, a clown's umbrella of red and purple tassels,
Sways in its green hanging pot outside our kitchen window
As I type you this letter. It's a mid-June of speedwells
In profusion on our lawn, wild mint and pussytoes
(That ridiculous name!)—and in our tulip trees and poplars,
Blue jays, cardinals, plovers, English sparrows
Live out their wild deliberate lives.... It rained
An hour ago but now the sun's come out again.

II

You know each living thing affects all others. Fruit flies
Forced by scientists to grow an extra pair of wings
Pass on that trait. But, months later, double pairs
Of wings appear on that same species taken at a spring
Two hundred miles away—in percentages that raise
Eyebrows, dampen foreheads. Crystallizing
Shapes, perhaps ideas, share the morphogenic fields,
Cocoons of mystery in which our planet's held.

III

That's from my reading, with a little of me thrown in
To ease the Latinate. More and more, I think we're here
Inside a spell, a universal hologram begun
With our agreement: bounce of the second laser
Off the first reflected beam. It's in the pattern
Of the interference where the gray squirrels slur
Across the roof and down the latticework
Behind the fuchsia, search and nibble, then scoot back.

IV

I think of you often, of your evening jogs, your arms
Zipzapping like a robot's as you lift the pace
Higher and higher, in that park where fountains brim
With leaves and old gum wrappers, and the face
Of Che Guevara stares from a mural by the dim
Light of a street lamp near the ornate underpass
You say is a tunnel of death for junkies, prostitutes.
I hope you've veered off, taken a safer route.

V

I remember, in your park, the faded yellow boats
For hire, the lovers and the tourists and the families
On the evening lake, how Monet it was; the harmonica notes,
Mike-amplified, that hung in the air: apostrophes
Over contractions. Everything about us seemed remote
And near at once, as in love and dreams and other mysteries
We've talked so long about and got so nowhere with,
Certain only of our world's alternatives.

VI

Clouds within clouds within clouds. Yet as I write,
The faucet drips, the refrigerator hums. I was woken
This morning by a great loud gang of crows. They lit
In the trees, on the lawn, on the wall, and finally when
My sleep was completely destroyed, took broad flight
Across the swaying fields. Does anything ever happen
The way we suppose? Is it our suppositions
Which change the patterns from what might have happened?

VII

Who knows? Who knows what we are, and why—and why
Our purpose is so clouded? Che Guevera,
Laminated photographs on cemetery stones, the sky
Filled with crows, our aging unto death, this algebra
Unsolvable? I type this letter. One day, you'll reply
With other images. I type and watch the fuchsia
Sway in its hanging pot...the squirrels. I gather
Information for you but I cannot make it clear.

VIII

Relax to Time and it will teach you, says an old
Zoroaster saying. Relax to your task and your task
Begins to show you what it wants. Let it hold
You in its easy grasp and fill the flask
With flowers cut from it—for the uncontrolled
Arrangements are reflections of the arabesque
Patterns spinning our world.... Friend, these words are as
The doubled wings of those mutated flies.

ANOTHER KNOWLEDGE

Seven miles from Provincetown, on clear June nights
The summer I learned stars,
Lying on my back beneath the starfields
With my charts and pencil flashlight, learning the way

From the curve of the Big Dipper's handle to Arcturus,
Spica, and then across the sky
To Denebola, the guardians of Polaris,
And The Lyre and The Swan,

I would often close my eyes, resting them awhile,
Taking sips from a can of beer
As I thought of how impossible all this was,
This rented cabin, our summer upon the dunes,

Night after night, the sky like the underside
Of a billowing, glittering parachute
Suspended above us. Sometimes, we'd rise and walk
By the ocean for hours,

My birthsign, Leo, pawing into heaven,
The Northern Cross tipped over on its side,
And try to imagine the feel of Berenice's Hair
And meeting Ettairin in an afterlife

Or spaceship. Would his eye stare so at us?
Would he say, "Get back down there,
You puny things?" Half drunk on modest success,
We hid from the Future,

Pretending we didn't care if it destroyed
Or elevated us. In the cabin
A small thin-metal globe the owner's child
Had left or outgrown

Served as a bookend for a small collection
Of Pearl Buck and Taylor Caldwell;
A white piece of driftwood vaguely like a whale
Was nailed to the fireplace wall

And on the screened-in porch
Someone's beginning pieces from a sculpture class,
Not quite bad enough to throw away,
Were not quite displayed. That summer

I'd leave you sleeping to go out
Into the Great Square of the wings of Pegasus,
And climb and climb up through the Milky Way
Alone. I wanted to know

Something I could be sure of, something I could carry
Back to the city, hidden
As tiny explosions of light waves in the brain,
A map I could follow with no end in mind.

THE NARROW MIND

It lives in a small backwater, and it doesn't know
Much more than dragonflies and darning needles,
The plash and galump of a frog. What it wonders
Is how do I get through another day.
It feeds on what's been whispered to it
In secret meetings at dusk, and what's proclaimed
By flights of crows. It likes
Lying on a sunlit log or wading
To shore with its fellows—where it seeks
Places it hasn't any trouble squeezing into.
What it demands, the few times it demands,
Is never to be shaken. But if that happens,
It wants the right to reassert itself,
And will die for that right. You can find it
By heading west at sunset, its spot
Marked by bubbles rising to the surface.
The brighter you are, the more likely it will greet you
With suspicion, so to get close to it
You must tell it stories that it wants to hear.
If you would expand it, if you would lift it out,
First consider its age and if it's strong enough
To live anywhere else. Elsewise,
You either must row around it or overwhelm it
With goodness and mercy and bribes.

THE NEO-TRANSCENDENTALIST

He feels them travel through him: the nurse-practitioner,
Breasts swaying above her patients, her face restrained,
That he's never heard laugh; the product manager
Who showed him a house in a dream of foliage;
His daughter with a piece of broken glass
Who carved her thigh wide open, then just stared
Until she finally screamed; his out-of-courage
Best friend close to sobbing, drunk on Dewars

At a Long Island party. They travel through him. They take
High roads and low roads, run the rapids of his blood,
Picnic in his eyes. Camped at a spring-fed lake
Deep in his shoulders, they join with other travelers,
His parents, his in-laws, the stuttering pharmacist,
To whisper their stories. Off in an eastern woods,
New arrivals seem stunned, cup their hands and call
To mountains they aren't sure are there—a waist-high mist

Cutting their bodies. They're lost in him,
But don't know they're lost. To them, he's transparent,
A mood, a longing, something only sensed along the rim
Of an old darkened valley.... A woman from Memphis
Stands out in the rain, saying her father's name
Over and over.... Walking a wooden bridge, his aunt
Remembers a smallpox epidemic and the kiss
Of a child on her forehead. Who can he blame

If not himself for how they search his mind
For answers? All he has are images: this sunset
Over the missile silos of Montana; this unsigned
Letter nailed to a church door, and the photograph
Of bodies at Auschwitz tumbled like bloated jacks;
The LEM on the moon, black pajamas, a faint

Spiral of laughter as the travelers take a path
Into his heartlands. There, the wind blows thick

Clouds of soot and smoke across the interstates,
Hamlets and railroad tracks. One traveler slumps
In the darkness of a barn hayloft; another sits
Alone in a wheatfield, playing a harmonica
To hills so distant in the afternoon they might become
Milkweed puffs. The travelers drop gray ropes
Into his caverns, project *L'Avventura*
On the walls of his inner skin and drum

His fingers against his desk. When he speaks, their voices
Are upon his tongue: his wife praying hard, his son
Lip-synching rap music. They're so various,
So deep in his cells, so demanding, he feels he has no life
Left of his own. Or perhaps he never had
A life without them, and perhaps John Donne
Was right about islands.... The travelers drift
In and out of his sleep. He hears their glad

Shouts when they discover signs to nearby cities,
Their moans of pain and love. He looks, with them,
Toward a blanked-out heaven. Some he watches die
In old people's hospital cribs, or at the height
Of sexual frenzy, giving, receiving. Some turn into
Statues of hatred, thinking themselves damned,
Or groves of self-pity where each moonless night
They dance among themselves as they renew

Vows he's witnessed. Those few who escape,
Who skydive into the abyss in brilliant suits
And flowery dresses, who bleed out of his fingertips,
He never hears from again.... The nurse turns down

The sheets of her bed; the product manager
Whistles Noel Coward; his daughter loots
A seven-gable house for music and a wedding gown;
His best friend paints a peace sign on a subway car....

And who is he? And who is he to judge? Alone,
He would lie down in green pastures, listening
To flies and water-skeeters traveling upon
Moist air or still waters. Alone, he couldn't find
His countenance before him when he bent to drink
Or feel his muscles stretch, his tall voice sing
Ballades or madrigals. He'd fade to a single line
Of waves off Gay Head Beach, would drift and sink

Toward the nothingness of sand, particle, molecule,
Atom, meson, quark, out of consciousness
Into the incomprehensible before the longing will,
The human will imagined him—that simultaneous
Instant of fulfillment and desire: creating one
And the created one.... Each traveler has a choice,
He whispers to himself. I took that choice. How beautiful
It is to be mundane, alive, to not have to explain

Anything away.... The travelers climb spine steps
In him, breathe the scent of wintergreen. They read
His palms, they sound his groin, they keep
Caches of books beneath his belly-folds,
And one is preaching from the upper limbs
Of the oak in his collarbone, shouting out the need
Of travelers throughout this and other worlds
For maps and prayer sheets, for the rise and fall of rhyme.

AT BROWN

Mad John Berryman, who I walked home from class
To Edwin Honig's house
He'd rented for his raving on that year—
When was it? Sixty-four?—
Told me, "Son, don't ever win an argument
Without you say a prayer
You not be humble pie." Oh, in his cups
He could take a single line by Yeats
And huff and puff it so it sang and sang
Like a bejesused thing. At the gate
He turned and wagged a finger. Providence stretched out
Below us, Christmas lights
Just coming on. And Kate came to the door
In a blue, blue dress. "When we go away,
The telephone won't ring." I saw him last
Gathering his children in his arms.
Poor mad John, poor goose, poor Tiny Tim;
Dear Poetry, the losses you sustain.

STILL WATERS

No matter how deeply they run, no matter
    how you have been led here beside them,
watching the crow's shadow, the water-skeeter's ride
    across their filmy surface; no matter
how many have drowned in them, thinking their lily pads
    green stepping stones upon the face of time,
no matter. You are at their banks now,
    sketchpad discarded, the sound of rapids
so far behind you it is deer feet on the leaves
    in an old maple forest. No matter
who you have loved, or stolen from, or murdered,
    rest here. The cradle of Moses
lies hidden in these rushes, Monet's muted palette
    drifts within reach—and the frog prince sleeps
on that glittering log. If you look down
    through your reflection, knowing it is false,
you may see the dragon stretching out its claws
    that rake heaven for rain, or Ophelia's tresses
golden among the weeds. Or you may find
    nothing but minnows nosing in the sunbeams' latticework,
a turtle coming up for air, its reptile's head
    in almost blind swaying. No matter. Take off your sandals,
lie on your back, breathe deeply, but with no
    purpose in mind. You are a sparrow's wing,
you are a psalm. Beside the still waters,
        you will be restored.

TALKING WITH POETS

Gossip is most of it, a barrier of thorns and small berries
Cultivated to disguise a wall,
False entrances and gates with shallow courtyards behind them,
And sometimes a few gypsies slowly dancing in firelight
Or swinging pails as they take a path down through the forest
To an old mossy well. Small heaps of masks,
And costumes with puffy sleeves or threadbare blouses
Lie beside the moat, are rummaged through
As often as not. But the poets seldom talk
Of forays they've taken; although they are always riding
In and out, mounting or dismounting, holding
The traces, wiping their brows and calling
For strong drink and friends, their verbal reports
Are sketchy, reluctant. No, they would rather laugh
Than speak of high rooms and the maiden's cot,
Books on stone shelves, what shackled prisoners
They may have been shown.... Yet if all this sounds
Too romantic, consider the cop coming home
To his house in the suburbs, how he pretends
There are no city streets until he walks their shadows;
Or the bored-to-death businessman,
The void he plunges daily, rising out of it
Like a circling, wounded hawk, blood under his nails
And in his throat, seeking Lethe
In television comedies or children's homework grades;
Or the doctor who vanishes
Into a nightmare of tumors, splintered bones,
The cardiographic line of a dead horizon,
CAT scans and mottled skin, before she finds herself
Whispering for the mercy of an airplane above layered clouds,
Flirtation, oblivion.... Still, if only the poets
Would cease in their talk of grants and reputation,
Reviews, or lack of them, readings, teaching loads,
Editors and enjambment, then on an autumn evening

17

When the wall is a looming thing of masonry,
Bulwarks and turrets, and a king walks by himself
Under limpid banners, how I would love to hear
(for I have read their books, and like you marvelled),
Of the way they find Blue Sailors by a country road,
Wander in Sibelius, or how they've taught their lines
To study a landscape starting with morning sunlight
Coasting the grass. Talking with poets,
I could be enthralled by cries of Russian wolves,
The smell of vanilla flavoring in an open brown bottle,
What happens when they look at statesmen's eyes—
If only they were not so distrustful, so afraid, so exhausted,
So bent on saving themselves for the perfect man or woman
Who will listen to their voices in another time
More living to them now than these roses, these open palms.

THE SAME RIVER, TWICE

Carefully, they entered it again, expecting
something to quake, or vanish, or beat its wings
as in the son and father paradox
of time travel stories. They expected
a house where a stand of maples swayed
in the warm August wind, a drifting rowboat
out toward the center, graffiti on the boulders
where the river curved slightly, then gentled
over light and dark pebbles, their game of *Go*
still unresolved. But even the slant
of sunlight was the same, the green rushes,
the turtle's bronze upon that mossy log,
and a cardinal's red flash precisely at
the moment a white mare in the meadow opposite
trotted, then galloped. The same current pulled
vaguely, like thoughts in a church book,
or an English shepherd's lute. They stirred the same
armada of floating willow leaves,
the same dark sand that rose in small tornadoes
with each step they took. She had lifted, that day,
her lace skirt to her knees; he remembered
how she'd looked like she would curtsy,
and his smiling at that.... The flat stone he skipped
hopped the same five, six, *seven* times, then sank.
She had laughed then and now she laughed again,
the physics of the thing impossible. Was this
only memory, he wondered, false at that,
an eddy, a singularity? He watched the river
flowing about them, its calm, each rippled facet
a slightly more blurred hologram
of all that they were. Consciousness, surely;
the oilcloth feel of lily pads; warmth, then cold,
then warmth again. He skipped another stone.
Her hem dropped to the water as it had before,

molding around her ankles, and she shivered
in all this wonderful impossibility,
while the crow flew over, the mare on the bank
trotted once more, the old river slipped away.

CITIES OF THE FIFTIES (A GLOSE)

for Frederick Feirstein

Cities were harmonies, vast orchestras
You could spend a whole day walking through
Among thin upper tones and deep down gutty basses,
Up Beggar Street, down Bullet Avenue.
Providence, Schenectady, and Denver
Drew us to their notes, their weaves
Of rich and poor, the Malamud grocery store
Shopped by a millionaire,
Flag-draped bridges, bargains you would not believe,
Glimpses of white bras
Between blouse buttons of a thousand Eves.
We wore our hearts upon a thousand sleeves,
Hoots and catcalls mixed with our applause:
Cities were harmonies, vast orchestras.

Dayton, Boise, Memphis, Santa Fe—
Each had a different sound and resonance;
In one, a love triangle, a piccolo café,
While in another cymbals turned to clay.
Each evening ended in a ballroom trance.
But every city we took Trailways to
Turned out a different audience,
A regional accent, strange cop beats, a tribal dance,
A long Chicago sob, New Orleans hullabaloo
You could spend a whole day walking through.

Day and night we wandered them alone:
Uptown, downtown, across the railroad tracks
Into their pits, then up their high trombones,
Flutes and oboes to the old brownstones
And civic monuments—to hear the trumpets
Of Seattle, Albuquerque's drumming paces,
To lie in New York's fields of clarinets,
Or pluck Miami strings, press thumbs to Pittsburgh frets,

And find, dear God, those still-believing faces
Among thin upper tones and deep down gutty basses.

Sheet music rain of Bangor, street corner Hays violins,
Patches of foggy oboes and bassoons,
Harps in Charleston's tenements, the tuba taxi spins
Past Little Rock's gray window mannequins,
Cincinnati restaurants, Atlanta afternoons:
The riot wonderful.... And in the news
A mix of minor dissonance and whistling tunes,
Preludes, overtures, immigrant tycoons,
Conductors bowing, pigeons flying, Old welcoming the New
Up Beggar Street, down Bullet Avenue.

A SHORT HISTORY OF THE VIETNAM WAR YEARS

Nothing was said until the house grew dark
And a fishnet of stars was cast upon its windows.
In the tall bedroom mirror, the door to Watergate
Opened again. A helicopter tiny as a moth
Flew across the lovers' flanks, its slow pinwheel blades
Making the sound of grief and churning rivers.

Placards lifted, the marchers of the Sixties
Stood in green meadows. Then folksongs began
Rising from their lips like blue leaves in summer
And time was a slipstream where a Phantom jet
Rolled in the sun. The lovers ran their hands
Over the rice fields and the panting oxen.

Deep in itself, the bedside clock unwound
By the edge of a pool, casting its minutes out
To a shoal of Destroyers. *Be still,* the lovers whispered.
In the room above the hall a mud-stained jeep
Backed up to a wooden brothel in Saigon,
An orange-robed monk knelt down in billowed flame.

The lovers grew sad. A soft rainy wind from Ohio
Brushed gunfire bursts and tear gas over them.
We will never love money, they said, clinging to each other,
Or dress like television, work like I.B.M.
We will grow flowers to slide into rifle barrels,
And we will dance barefoot on Wall Street's glass chin.

That was when hope was a temple bell, a bleeding eye,
A circle of books around the lovers' bed
As the soldiers looked on. Mai Lai fell half-asleep
Under the full thrust moon. On bruised hands and knees,
Tet advanced along the shadowed railroad ties,
And the deltas awoke and flooded Washington.

We will drift to Cambodia, the lovers said,
Dance in People's Park, burn incense tapirs
At Buddhist shrines. The house wrapped its black armband
Over the lovers as they lay entwined.
And if you listened, you could hear the mortar fire
Walking up the valleys like an old blind man.

THE REPORT

The wind is blowing on the prison walls
Above the secret towns. In the secret towns
Men are walking through the streets with guns.

Men with guns are walking through the streets
Below the prison walls. The prison walls
Are on the cliffs above the secret towns.

Behind the shattered windows and the shattered doors,
The women kneel and pray. The women pray
While men are walking through the streets with guns.

Men with guns are walking through the streets,
Breaking down the doors. Breaking down the doors
Is what the men do in the secret towns.

The women pray they'll stop. Please stop, they pray,
And let the prison fall. Let the prison fall,
They pray behind the windows and the shattered doors.

But the men are laughing in the secret towns,
And carrying the guns. The men with guns
Walk and laugh below the prison walls.

Below the prison walls lie secret towns
With broken doors. Beyond the broken doors
Men are walking through the streets with guns.

THROWING CAUTION TO THE WIND

If it wasn't that her body weighed so much
more than a paper cutout, if we could have grasped
her ankles and under her armpits and lifted her
easily upwards, swung her lightly out
over the cliffs and watched her spin and whirl
like a loosened sail, like a newspaper page,
we would have done it earlier. If she hadn't
given us her list of a thousand reasons
why we wouldn't succeed beyond our normal lives,
hadn't blown in our ears, brought us birthday cakes
with too many candles, smoothed her skirts demurely
as she sat at our table and refused the wine,
we might have known her plan was to deceive us
with tiny kisses, fingers on our wrists, shy looks
instead of promises. Not for her
the spontaneous gesture, the nudist beach, the TV set
so large it overwhelms the room,
wild walks in the rain, *menage à trois*, great anger
fully expressed, jumps into dirty politics.
"No," she whispered, "no, I can't"—content
with her tea and her placemats.... So when at last
we found the parchment maps where four winds blow
from four far corners, their crimson cheeks swelled,
eyes bulging, tempests upon the high seas,
we struggled and lifted and tossed her from us,
only to behold her writhing, her clothes torn off,
as stretching upwards in a ballerina's stance,
she blew out of our sight. From that day on,
we've ridden constantly among the whales
and watched the stormy petrels flicker wave to wave.
        We've called the gods down,
outrageously sporting with them until the time
(and we know it will happen; we can read the signs)
Caution shall return to us, her amnesiac face

dull as a window shade, her thin lips pursed in dread,
and damn us, damn us, we will tend her wants
as she takes the chair by the fire and strokes the kitten,
looking around her, knowing what is best,
the formal manner, the elegant way of the house.

ON THE NEW HAVEN LINE

This is the day you might have died
And never heard a newsboy's cry again,
Or looked out from the window of your train.
This is the day you might have died.

This is the day news might have flown
By letter, telegraph, or telephone,
To friends from Stony Brook to Riverside.
This is the day you might have died.

This is the day you might decide
To visit Croaton Heights or Sally's Lane.
Because, today, you might have died,
No matter what you lose, you gain.

This is the day you might have died
From natural causes, accident, or suicide:
No more adventures in the great unknown
Of hollyhocks and knucklebone.

This is the day. You might have died
And never seen Rowayton in the rain
Or morning glories bloom in Darien.
This is the day you might have died.

IN THE VALLEY OF THE SHADOW OF DEATH

I

Descended into it, we catch our breath
    and tap our compasses. The light is from Poe,
misty and pale with rivulets of thought
    crossing back and forth, cataract-eyed,
and in this light, the path we take along the valley floor
    wavers sometimes, yet sometimes becomes so clear
we see each tree root, every random stone.

Mostly, we go single file, unroped and wordless,
    the bodies before us and the bodies afterwards
motions and gutturals, oddly jerking shapes
    we almost forget have names. The valley walls
are steep and smell of doused campfires.
    Boulders fall through the ferns. Mornings,
we count ourselves. Someone's always gone.

To where, we don't know. We think we hear them
    climbing a long ways away, or their swimming strokes
in a river or pond, or in that dream-shout,
    that popped ear, that single Winchester rifle crack
waking us to nothing but that they are missing,
    the soft wind in the spruce, a barracked night bird,
overanxious raccoon with its tiny stealing paws.

Sometimes, we discover a valley town
    long deserted, gray splintered railroad ties
framing its gardens. Rust. Sepia autumn fields,
    crosses as lonely as those at Little Big Horn,
a Phillip Larkin church with its clapperless bell.
    A woman will put a sprig of heal-all in her hair,
a man will break into a little song.

II

In such a town, in a mansion old as Moses,
    I found glass-littered parlors, bannistered stairs,
cobweb curtains in its many rooms, dust, dust.
    Blown lightbulbs, singed from inside,
hung over each bed, their light cords frayed.
    Stained washbasins sat on splintered dressers.
Rotted clothes lay wadded in each corner.

I swung my lantern from the highest balcony
    that could take my weight. I yelled
out into the fog, but no one answered,
    all of us searching for ourselves, exploring
buildings we fancied. Here and there, I saw
    other lanterns swaying in the dusk:
Richard Brautigan tales, the girl upon the bridge.

We have all lost someone. Last afternoon,
    we skirted a waterfall; last evening, an owl
with its curious New Age face flew over us.
    At night, swamped by the stateship bulk
of a dark mountain peak, someone whispered
    a poem about pride. We are walking
from God knows where into God knows what

will befall us. Think of a shrouded world,
    Think of how we overcome our fright,
grow weaker and weaker, footsore, our shortwave radios
    useless this far down beneath the shadow.
Interference night and day. Sphere music
    only coming through in a word or phrase,
ellipses, Sappho fragments, all transmission garbled.

Power lost. Useless telescopes. Tree markings
    obscured by new growth. Vines grow heavier. We take
turns at the point. It's all political
    we sometimes believe. At other times, we praise
any who stand alone among the branches
    hacking their way, amateurs who don't give up,
sweating and cursing those whom we'd anointed

leaders and saints. Is anyone searching for us?
    Is anyone up there on the cliffs? Is space
really as black as they say and stars as bright
    in the tent that's our reverse? *Oh Jesus,
the wind and the rain.* I feel my way
    only by my hands and intuition
there will be an end to this I can accept.

But only the Valley remains. Even vultures
    lose their sense in it. A ladybug
in its Stendhal red and black goes wandering
    down the light green center of a dark green leaf
glowing in the mist and dew, and then
    like a confetti dot is taken up
by a gust from the hidden pass we cannot find.

        III

I will fear no Evil, we all said,
    for Thou art with me. I will be comforted
by thy rod and thy staff. Yet no one warned us
    it would be this hard. Lately, I'm remembering
too much for too long. When we stop for rest,
    shapes in the mist grow more and more distinct.
If I close my eyes it might be I can touch them.

It might be. However, the log or rock
   on which I'm sitting grows uncomfortable
or a blister requires care. In a few more hours
   I'll be bedded down beside dark embers,
dreaming of rapids. Now, I rise again,
   trying to accept my lot, this life as it is,
the presence of my enemies, the oil and cup,

that the house of the Lord may not welcome me
   with all of my doubts. If I could send
only one short message somehow back to you,
   today, as we go lower, I keep constructing
what it would be. Images, I guess,
   how we walk for ages with our faces set
or loosening, how many of us there were,

our bare arms, our knapsacks, the way
   one of us whistles, one of us cries,
all of us stumble. Whether or not
   there is a shepherd and we are his flock,
goodness and mercy, or hatred and revenge,
   I've stood by glades where elk browse out of darkness,
I have wet my lips with anxious love,

and standing in a place of leaves and hail,
   recited a Chinese poem as Pound rendered it
to empty forest land, the words themselves
   falling and rising, the compass spinning, yet
held. We are here to witness. We are here
   to trick our voices into praising God.
In Death's shadow we have found our own.

M.F.A.

for Sarah Collings

Troubled by many things, she stands beneath a streetlight,
thinking this might be an Agatha Christie story,
if this were England. But it's New York
near Columbia, the spires of St. John's Cathedral
half visible in the rainy morning, a subway train
somewhere below her, bringing all those passengers
to destinations she can only guess about. Well then,
she says, snapping her fine head back, things to be done,
things to be questioned. *Gargoyles.* She must know
more about gargoyles, rose teacups, that man
who seems to be watching her from another dimension
veering toward hers. She takes a few strides, pauses,
as dollar umbrellas rise up around her like bubbles
in a twig-clotted stream. A woman gaunt from AIDS, she supposes,
stands in the doorway of a Burger King,
both hands extended, palms up, as if wearing handcuffs,
and the sidewalk used book seller covers his sad
out-of-date textbooks, underlined Penguin editions,
in plastic tarp, huddles beneath his windbreaker.
Can you read, she wonders. So much, so much
to know, to discover. The only way to survive
must be to just go on. *Little towns of Indiana,*
who lives there? And does the wind really sleep
under a pigeon's wing? She blinks, several times,
and for only an instant feels herself entrapped
in a deep pine forest, a black owl's silhouette
above her. *Lang's theory that we all go mad*
at least three times a day. Recalling it comforts her,
and she hums a little of "Rule Britannia"
and "the rain in Spain falls mainly on the plain"
as she steps ahead briskly. In her mind, a scene
with a piano background—Vaughan Williams, she believes—
begins to form. There's a country lane, a herd
of crossing sheep, a vicarage, an old mossy cemetery,

footsteps behind her.... And then the words come,
strong, almost knocking her down, the phrases,
sentences, whole paragraphs, and she hangs onto them
tightly, how dear they are, how wonderful,
yet almost dark, like the sound of a thousand barely ringing bells
in Dover's deep tides. But she'd better get on. The rain
comes down harder as she heads toward her workshop,
black hair streaming wet, thin dress clinging
to her body's light curves. *Hey lady, hey lady,*
a street-vendor calls. *You want to save my life?*

THREE A.M.

Downstairs, a glass on the kitchen table
Suddenly breaks. A woman wakes in pale darkness
And, rubbing beads of moisture from her bedside window,
Stares out at the snow.

The large wishbone of a leaping hare
Crosses her yard
Then disappears behind a metal shed,
And what she's chosen every year to be

"The last leaf"
Still hangs from an elm branch. Every year,
The same. Every year
She wakes like this, to her dead husband's breathing

In the empty space beside her,
His ambitions and passions
The small things she now knows they were,
And cries, "Why leave me? Damn you, damn you!",

The bed see-sawing with her grief. From the road,
The sound of snow-chained tires
Mixed with the wind. She lifts the wooden sash
Enough to plunge one hand and then her whole arm from it.

And this is what we see in the winter night
As we turn in her driveway, lost,
Our highbeams flooding the house,
Catching her hand, holding it in the light.

PARENTS SUPPORT GROUP

Our children half-lost, we gather at the table,
Making small polite jokes
About weather and coffee. The blinds are drawn.
Outside, the summer afternoon is tennis strokes,

A grackle calling to its mate, windchimes,
Sliding tailgates of delivery vans. Long-timers smile
And pat the new arrivals' backs. Our therapist
Takes a long, long, long, long, *long* while

Before he starts, reluctantly. That hot potato, Pain,
Goes round and round the table. Who of us
Are blameless, who share blame
For why our children left a crust

Of blood across their wrists, gulped pills, or think
Their terribly thin bodies still are fat,
Did drugs, did drink
Behind ripped billboards of their raw self-hate?

We don't know. Weeks...or was it days ago,
Self-tucked in the illusion we control
Our lives...sane, in our accepting this...we thought
That all stones roll

Downhill, all rabbits leap, the months ahead
Are simply spaces on our calendars
Where plans are penciled or not penciled in.
That's normal and not wrong.... But now we're here

Talking with strangers. To our left
The lady in a green dress weeps; the man
Whose daughter must be begged or bribed to eat
Keeps putting up and putting down his hand,

Then polishing his glasses on his paisley tie.
I don't know what to say. I don't know anything
That can help us all. Words alone
(How many words there were!) have come unstrung

And scatter everywhere. Back in their halls
Our children hunch above their Scrabble board,
Or shoot the breeze
As aimlessly as they shot down our world.

ODE TO THE COLD WAR

I

A faint light blinking in the Bering Strait,
The dead face of a Russian boy, the spy
Never returned from Berlin—these were yours;
And body bags, Chinese horns, the pounding shoe,
    A riderless horse in Washington,
Turning radar screens beneath an arctic sky,
Yours, yours. In you, the State triumphant,
        Rambo, Big Brother,
        MacArthur, Eisenhower,
        Stalin, the Politburo,
French bodies hanging on the wires at Dien Bien Phu,
    Space, Time, Chaos, satellites,
    Kindergarten children
    Hiding under desks, Castro,
A thousand missiles rising from their buried silos.

II

In you, *The Gulag Archipelago*
Took its windswept shape; Neil Armstrong
Stepped upon the moon. As your governments
Raged over him, the peasant in the field
Could hope for freedom or equality, not both,
        But either choice
Better than the hopelessness he felt
Landless, penniless, voiceless, while the rich
    Danced in mansions filled
    With songs he could have sung,
    Rose arbors that he could have leaned upon,
Tasting the wine, talking of the truth,
        The voting booth,

Were he not poor, uneducated, sprung
From serfs and slaves and brutal legacies.
Your fingers reaching from the cold, you promised him
If he would die for you, that history
Would lift his children to a street of gold.

III

Thing of walls, thing of barriers, thing of parallels,
Of caves and steppes and slums and jungles,
      Thing of withering away,
      Of straying aircraft, tracer fire,
Mushroom clouds and cancer wards,
Airlifts, Disneyland, ill-shaved McCarthy,
Blacklists and defections, K.G.B.,
      CIA, SANE,
      MIGs, Phantoms,
Tanks turning back toward Hungary,
Thing of suspicion, hatred, body snatchers,
      Shortwave radios,
Interrogation, Orwell, streams of refugees,
      Doctor Zhivago,
Crete, Chernobyl, and the great economies
Bound to you. Thing of waking up in Leningrad,
Chicago, New York, London, Paris, Budapest,
    Moscow...or in a tiny shed
Deep in the Urals or Louisiana bayous,
And you there, you always in your place
With your equivalent of twenty tons
      Of TNT
For every human on the planet's face:
First strike, second strike, and then
      Oblivion....

IV

You organized our lives. You made our sacrifices
    Possible. With you, we could forgive
The empty shelves, the shoddy stores,
    Learn to ignore
The homeless pushing shopping carts, the poor
    Slouched in Grand Central,
Shrug our shoulders at the Trumps and Brodskys,
    Museums, dachas,
    Crack, cocaine,
    Savings & Loan,
    TV Guide, People.
Umbrellas of defense would rise above us,
Star Wars would protect us,
And Reagan would shine on through history.
    The poor deserve their misery,
    Praise heavy industry,
May Day parades, the Fourth of July,
    The Internationale,
Jack London, Yevtushenko, Voznesensky,
    Steinbeck, Abram Tertz
("What is to be done?" wrote Tolstoi),
Bourgeois, proletariat, and democrat,
    Republican Capitalist pigs,
    Communist dogs.
You helped us as we pulled the fallen logs
    Across Siberia,
You laid out in the Harlem slums,
In crime-mugged streets, in Selma, Alabama.
    You had come
From Hobbes and Locke and Marx and Engels
    Against dictatorships,

To kiss our fervent lips
And save us from confronting what was real.

V

Among the cemetery tombs of Leningrad,
A souvenir seller lays his cap aside
And openly prays: *Comrade, comrade,*
Do not regret the cause for which you died.
All of us die for causes, large and small,
Silly and noble. History gloves our hands,
Clothes us in its uniforms and clouds our minds,
Leads us to or leaves us where we fall.
The great snows come. The cold war ends,
Warm bloody fingers crack the window blinds.

VI

And this your epitaph:
For fifty years you froze us in your path.
And now no more
Lake Placid miracles, Nadia's theme,
Whittaker Chambers, Alger Hiss,
The Rosenbergs,
Smuggled manuscripts, the Marshall Plan,
"Ich bein ein Berliner,"
Profumo scandal,
Wiretapping Hoover,
James Bond, Samantha Fox—
All jumbled, all confused: John Glenn,
Yuri Gagarin,

The Bay of Pigs, sold orphan children,
    Chile overthrown, Che Guevara killed,
        The iron curtain,
    Cement and Hemingway,
    The Bolshoi Ballet,
Tribes, religions, nationalities
Held together for the greater cause;
The advertisers' and the lawyers' paradise
    Of twisted laws,
Leaving in their wake our shattered
        Ships of state
        Ice-bound no more,
The reign of selfishness supreme.
            How you entertained us,
            How you toyed with us,
        How you betrayed us,
How you left us empty in your empty husk.
        "Ask not
What your country can do for you,
But what you can do for your country."
        "Workers of the world unite,
        You have nothing to lose but your chains"—
Cacophony, faded cacophony,
        Cast votes,
        Flute notes,
I sing the Song of Myself.

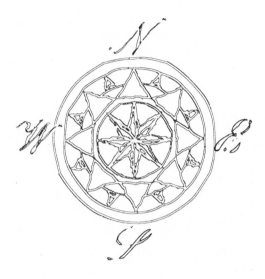

FROM
Anon and Various
Time Machine Poems
AND
Regions with
No Proper Names

TO A WOMAN HALF A WORLD AWAY

Just about now
you will be dusting the flowers
or changing from your bathrobe into something nice.

The kids will all be out
oiling their bikes, and thinking of birthdays.
The mailman will take his time up the hill.

Maybe this is the morning you will go shopping
to buy a percolator, or a yellow blouse.
Drive, darling, careful.

That book you mean to read
if nothing on the set is well worth watching,
I bet is something with an ending really happy.

Now you are dressed
and walk around the house with your blood pressure up,
looking for something, anything, not in its place.

The mailman comes, and this letter
of course is not there.
You worry just a little as you close the door.

And then you turn, and your face
is just so beautiful it makes me stop
and wonder why I thought I would remember your body.

Here, you will remember, I am in night
beside a river that seems to flow through every field,
learning I am sentimental past my wildest fears.

AT THE PHOTOCOPY MACHINE

Another miracle. How many can he stand?
He used to look for unexpected parks
on off-streets of the city—
a few iron benches where the secretaries tanned.

Once or twice a year he'd find
a cat's-eye marble in a dusty room
or in the corner of a used car lot
and pick it up, and pocket it for luck.

Sometimes, when her mood was right,
his wife would wantonly
behave experimentally,
display a wild sex savagery;

and now and then throughout
the year, there'd be a night
of perfect television, and the good
unread books would lie about

the house. But watching this
useful, sleek, incomprehensible machine
operating like the DNA
molecule of sheer efficiency

he worries for the children, sees
them laughing at the little rocket ships
which drop against the moon,
and all the duplicates

of Balboa, Marco Polo, Velazquez,
who are to come. He lifts
the papers from the metal tray
and wishes there were missionaries still

trekking toward the outposts of
some unenlightened continent cut off
by mountains from the inescapable
waves which bring the same

faces, forces, miracles to all
the wooden, metal, tube, and glass
sets that have survived
the curse of the secrets of one.

POSTER POEM

The eight flames look
like petals of a hybrid rose
blown skyhigh
        orange, red,
animated by
someone from the world of Nulla-A.

He runs up an Earth
craterless—
black, black, black.

Your strange clothes burn:
The cape. The psychedelic blouse. The pants
large at the ankles.
"Don't be unholy," you said
raw between gossip.
"We were such freaks
to survive—
        yon spasm
           of light."

He runs
through your teleprobe.
        SUPPOSE
THEY GAVE A WAR
...AND NOBODY CAME
you read

—so adult, artful in
your guilt
—and bought it, put it up
with masking tape,

stripped down, lay down,
in bed.

The moon was breaking off from Earth again.

PROPHECY

The horses spiral on that great gone dim
that was whatever was his brain. Nero ends
his life: *la fin du monde arrivera.*

"Whereas, the end of the world is approaching,"
royal proclamations began, "ye shall know
a pilgrimage has sent us to the Holy Land."

And the year one thousand was a year the sea
would give up all the dead that were within it.
Bernard, a visionary, saw the end of man.

There was a reign of pleasure; maidens danced
by firelight, for in Babylon the Antichrist
was born. In showers of blood, panic and prayer.

After that the famine: the unbeliever dies
at the foot of the cross. Starving children enticed
by an egg. One was burned for selling flesh

in the marketplace. Another who dug
for corpses—he was also burned alive.
De la Fin du Monde..., wrote a saint.

It went on. Stoffler said the planets would meet
in the constellation of Fish. The peasants ceased
to cultivate their fields. No debts were paid.

Nostradamus penned his astrological joke.
A total solar eclipse sent many French
to wait it out in their cellars, warmed and perfumed.

Halley's comet came and went, and would come
again. Crazy Californians
spent a night on a mountain the year

the bomb was dropped. In 1962
Khetu joined five planets, and the sun and moon.
The serpent Rahu swallowed the sun.

And still we live. I have a four-eyed friend
who says his boat to Australia was
loaded with Americans.

And I myself, when the Russian ships
toward Cuba steamed, took three days off,
cleaned up my basement, and stocked up on food.

La fin du monde arrivera. Well, why not?
Since Nero fiddled, I can fiddle, too.
The horses spiral on that great gone dim.

A NEW AGE

We walk into a new age
carrying knapsacks, twin sleeping bags.

The colors of the trees slightly turn.
We have stepped from one photograph
into a print almost but not quite perfect.

Your voice has a small new tone
to it; I feel
a slight new texture when I touch your hand.

I am not sure if this age
is darker or lighter.
The sun appears smaller,
shadows in the pines seem looser.

We do nothing to adjust. We walk a mile
and the difference goes forever.

I was thinking of having married another woman.
You were thinking of having married another man.

We lie down in the shade
of an oak with faded initials carved
ten feet up its trunk. Nothing, you say,
is wrong. It is just a new age.

THE COMING OF THE FIRST AEROPLANES

The coming of the first aeroplanes
out across America
obsesses me,
as other men are obsessed
by the President's face,
bi-sexual wives,
and I think *throttle stick, loop,*
barnstorm, goggles, dive,
shade my eyes
and all the doors
of all the houses open, and upon the small
lawns of 1920, people stand
praising God.
Satellites, the Venus probe, rim world,
teleport, dwarf stars, the luxon wall,
quasars, planetfall. I am
the first pilot from Boston.
Seeing a boy in a field,
I wave from the cockpit,
dip low my wings.
Aeroplanes.
    They called them
crosses in the sky.

THE PRESENT

The present is such a lovely place
that sparrows fly through it
and sunlight shines into it, day after day;
folk hymns are sung in it; out
in Nebraska two children
toss a softball back and forth;
sighing, a lovely woman
lies back in the present with her thighs apart,
adoring her lover;
men lean from
open car windows; they watch
the present go by
their lives, other lives, and they think
of swimming in April.
Into the present
comes a quietness. The stars
begin to replenish;
it is a summer evening on the planet Earth,
fireflies jounce in the darkness,
crickets, tree frogs. You never
knew such contentment.
Strolling, thoughts to yourself,
you feel the present is a valley, a refuge,
a compromise
between past and future,
and toss a stone at the river,
race your own life to your door.

KEATS

When you come down out of wilderness
everyone looks crazy,
even your friends look crazy.
I can't explain it. Everyone looks crazy.

One night, lofted up there,
we crawled from our sleeping bags, tent,
mosquito netting, and stood
under stars like white fine print

on a black page slightly bent
over us, and the moon
was a well of pale yellow light
and the planets unborn.

We stood on the world like two
acrobats who have learned
to balance themselves on a big
circus ball, while it turned,

and then we were nothing but people,
with no culture, no gods.
America fell, beyond us;
around us was fog, or clouds—

no matter. There was no reason
to live or to perish;
a bird sang off in the woods
or a nightingale sang in the forest.

THE DAY AFTER JUNE

I have been to Madness; it is a house
strongly built, not created.
It looks not at all like The House of Usher
and has been freshly painted.

All the others left when I came there,
drove away in carriages with high-rimmed wheels;
in my bedroom was a lopsized painting,
a pencil, a stone, a box of one-inch nails.

I sat down on the stairs and wrote
about the cobwebs flickered in the wind,
the dark replenishment of love,
the sun, the sun, the sun, the sun.

Nothing reached me there, not politics,
nor arms sawed off, not images
of women with soft dresses on, not friends
who knew the cure for curing agonies.

I had a television and I had my scotch,
two dreams—though one was deathly ill;
sufficient cigarettes, an essay book
including Faulkner saying mankind shall prevail.

In the kitchen, there was food enough;
the water faucets and the toilets worked;
a picture window stared into the sea—
Atlantic or Pacific—I don't remember which.

I remember writing up a storm
and sailing into it, my arms outspread.
Thinking that "a gentleness survives,"
I'd let myself be used and broken wide.

So here I was, in Madness, in the calm
room with draperies and wicker chairs;
I saw the Future coming down
into a place without me, without doors.

How did I leave? I left. That's simply all.
I left some zinnias in the upstairs vase,
did not shut the windows; set the phonograph
low volume and the tone control to bass.

I met the carriage coming through the trees;
the silent driver tipped his stovepipe hat.
The taste of poppyseeds was in my mouth;
the horses whinnied and the long whip cracked.

BRAINCHILD

He looks like one of those small creatures from
The Village of the Damned
and maybe he hates you
because you make it clear to him
he is not normal,
has not been brought here to waste any time
with matters like baseball
and has no business thinking
your wife is his mother. His function
is to speak with you,
to tell you what is in Shakespeare,
Fuller, and Peirce. If you give
him any time to himself,
he is expected to stay
in his crystal-clean room
working through madness.
Aware that he will never be allowed
to grow up and marry,
he becomes accustomed to his small
face and large eyes
and soon stops asking you
to describe
the world past your door.
If only you could love him. But he shrugs
all emotion away,
ticks off poetry
in the style of John Cage,
paints parallel lines.
Willed into being,
you cannot tell him to just disappear,
who cannot be lonely, afraid,
but will die when you die,
nameless, a brainchild,
an original.

THE STREET MYSTIC

Distinguished, he whispers you a plan
for catching field mice in a meadow of flowers.
His voice has the quietness of girls' voices
as they wilt and touch shoulders.
He stares at you, and you can't
tell if he is sincerely awakened
or mad
      or certainly harmless.
"We have built a monastery in the hills
outside America," he says,
"where the brothers and sisters
pray to candles and illuminated scrolls."
For many days after your meeting
his vision steps toward you from alleyways.
Vows of poverty, decisions to silence—
that strange life that you might have chosen,
he lives
      totally free from your childhood,
the way you enter darkness with no eyes.

WATER POEM

Today I became aware of water, stupidly—
as one becomes aware
of Death when the first wet sickness tears the body,
and Love when the radio makes sense at last.
Water. I close my eyes and sheets of it flood away
from the broom in my hand; specks of foam
drift from under the furnace, sweat loosens
my muscles. I drink from a blue water glass,
I walk to the mailbox in a black raincoat,
water pouring down; I use the bathroom; water splashes
out of my loins; I undress and bathe in water,
sink down to my chin; the mirror fogs.
I mop the cellar floor dry; I watch
late news of the storm: a child
is splashing from car to car in the swells
of water. Boats are half-capsized. I dream
of water, dream I am my father
swimming across a lake in the Adirondacks
under a full moon, too buoyant to drown.
I feel the water in my mouth, I hear
it drip from the faucet, drizzle leaf to leaf
in the beech tree outside the window.
Water. Waterfall. Water streaming down
the boulders. I am standing waist-high
on a rock in the ocean; it is raining hard.

A LAST MEMORY OF KOREA

When someone breaks apart
beside you, and you know
he could not swim deep,
had never touched the *Thresher*'s periscope
or filled his lungs
with water where the phosphorescent fish
amazingly sleep
or risked his life
cutting through wires,
explosive, days before
a standing army hit
the coral shore
and you suddenly surface in
the middle of a shopping center lot
so large it does not matter how you park,
around you are the lost Americans
walking toward
buildings, fountains, food,
racks of clothing; at
your elbow is
a lovely salesgirl who
wears fine perfume
and comes from Mississippi. It
was in the final days of Panmunjon,
someplace in that little country,
in that measured war.

WHEN YOUR SHIP COMES IN

You will be standing on the dock
with a coiled rope hanging from one shoulder
and the sea will smell blue.

You will half expect crowds,
reporters out of the 30's, dixieland bands,
but the only sound will be your ship approaching.

You will see it first as a tiny speck on the water
with dim running lights,
a white and black hull.

And then it will be there, before you—
a small ship but new—
looking as though it sailed in from the future.

You will try to be happy,
step down on the deck and take control,
remember you must try and thank the Lord.

But it will be so quiet, it will be so dark,
it was so long expected,
all night you will work quietly and not believe.

THE HORIZON

I have been looking out at the horizon
    all day, trying to discover perhaps a man walking
toward us, with a rifle clasped loosely in his hand;
    or a Conestoga wagon rolling out of the 1800's—
Sweet Betsy and the oxen carved from wood—
    or a battleship with all its deck guns blazing
and the kamikazes diving out of the sun;
    or a girl from the Horsehead Nebula who speaks
Celtic and is bringing us strands of a new religion;
    but there is only the horizon. Nothing moves
in the distance. No wind ripples the pines
    and the doors of the tiny houses do not open.
Even when I walk toward them, even when I run,
    nothing comes at me. There is the silence
of the horizon, the perfect calm of a line
    unbroken by the unfamiliar, wavering
in the afternoon heat. Below it
    Earth falls away, forever to Japan. The sky
is a blue wash to the stars. Whatever is beyond
    or might emerge from some tumblemeg dimension
does not emerge. The wet ball of the world
    spins the moon high above me. I stand
looking out at the horizon, for a train from Saratoga,
    a man descending a thousand library steps,
some action, some breaking, even a shark fin,
    some definite face shot with blood.

THE PERPETUAL MOTION MACHINE

Someone who has never heard of entropy
or Heisenberg is about
to make it come true:
a stupefying miracle of gears
spinning forever.
But for now it sits
in an attic or basement
needing only one
tiny adjustment—
a twist of a small socket wrench,
a tap,
and the world will be saved
by the tinkerer
who noticed how the stars
slide over Wisconsin,
always returning,
who had a good head on his shoulders, who read
a book on Edison.
Sometimes, walking by
a house from back before
the war with the Kaiser,
I look up, as if feeling
he was there watching,
and hear the strange humming
of the perpetual
      motion
      machine,
how peacefully, how endlessly, it stops.

THE LAMP STORE

It is hard to find shadows here:
light comes at us
from so many corners and angles.

So much light makes us cheerful; you smile
at an odd twist of steel,
a pool of red sparkles.

Huge silver pods of light
float on the ceiling.
Orange lampshades burst from the walls.

Such light! I look outdoors
through the one tiny window:
the autumn sky seems pale.

A few birds flutter
over the highway and maples.
Small lines of darkness

lean in from the west.
I turn back to your face,
expecting dark worlds.

But you shout, over the bright
tables of glass,
"Imagine working here! Imagine!"

I cringe back from your voice
as if light
can be broken like silence,

as if you could walk
down a hall
by climbing up stairs,

and open your robe,
be examined
by nothing but quiet

falling into the room
through the one open skylight
in a square on the floor.

"Whisper. Whisper," I say—
I am astonished
by even the quick

way your eyes flash,
the sudden energy which splashes
from all life, even my own.

66

FROM
OVERNIGHT IN THE GUEST HOUSE OF THE MYSTIC

JANES AVENUE

At the end of it, the school
that was once a museum: stairs from its second floor
led up to a huge locked door
and the reek, we imagined, of the missing mummy.

Get down from there,
our teachers—sad Depression things—
would shout. But we kept trying,
small shoulders pushing; hands on the pitted black knob.

They lied it wasn't there. We knew
as sure as we knew rowboats, wind and clouds,
in that cupola room, propped on a broken desk,
a mummy stood in brown-stained strips of cloth.

We hated them for lying. Oh, we knew, we knew
when the last bell sent us home, they gathered
by the door; the Principal unlocked it;
they entered and they gazed and they were shaken.

As we wished to be. The frogs that spewed
beneath our bicycles, the horseflies in the grass—
these were the small things they thought fit for us,
the happy children of Janes Avenue.

VARIATION ON A THEME
BY ERNEST HEMINGWAY

In a city where I once lived, for many years
an old man sat on his doorstep, in his hand
a brown facecloth, which he turned
over and over, smoothed out
against his knee, crumpled up, smoothed again,
then held at arm's length. Sometimes he buried
his whole face in it, and since he was dressed in tweeds
I could never decide
if he was Idiot or on his way to being wise,
or on his way back, the cloth
his rhodora. I never
asked; he never looked up
from his studies or madness, whichever
let him sit there every sunny day
thinking or not thinking. I never heard
anyone call him in; I never passed
his doorstep as he came out into the morning
or saw him sip from a glass, or even stand.

Like the streets and the marvelous pennies on sidewalks,
the iris that came out of nowhere,
he was a part of my days for a while and I trusted
him as only a question can be trusted,
never an answer
and I moved away from that city, never regretting
my silence or his
but missing the houses with the mansard roofs
and the tall brick chimneys, so red
against the snow falling, winters I lived there.

THE MYSTERY

for Prof. Israel Kapstein

I

Of course we hound it with words. To give it up
    to the trees and flat meadows
or the farmhouse that for thirty years has seemed
    about to topple into its deserted yard
would be, as Kapstein said, boring.

It is ours by right: both of long hunting
    and birth into knowledge. We have known
such moments! Such moments when the hills turn gray,
    and the wind has seemed to settle into itself
and it seemed to be solved, it seemed to be solved!

The moments of love: the hand across your own
    so briefly in time; the glance across a table
through candle flames like tiny leaves suspended
    in the soft darkness of a restaurant where each
wall is blue or mirrored. Such moments

the mystery seems to deepen and we follow it
    down, down, down until there is an end
to words, a living coral reef
    faintly glowing, extending to the ocean floor's
horizon, luminous fish like flattened raindrops twirling.

II

We cannot leave it alone, said Kapstein, even
    supposing we could, always it would be waiting
in the moment before you cross the room and look
    from the window to the sunlit hills you knew
would be sunlit, or the ordinary stars in heaven.

And the butler did not do it. From the start
   we were not misled by the Master's careful words
and the sweeping gowns of his ladies. We suspected
   something in the twilight, beyond the elms
and the light a moving picture of itself

on the outskirts of the garden. O, the mystery
   is bound to resist us, Kapstein said, our invention
of words that draw closer, curtain in the wind
   blowing in the farmhouse, footsteps in the yard,
what is discovered of our lives when we discover

how close we can draw, how near we can come
   without fainting. It is the gunshot
muted in the parlor; it is the room
   locked with a body inside; it is the clue we follow
like those hounds forever but not quite yet closing in.

KOREAN VETERAN

He noticed, at breakfast,
the tapered fingerbones and slightly curving nails
of icicles outside the kitchen window,
the knuckles and joints
of three days melting and freezing:
a skeleton's hand
hanging disembodied in the sun,
and tried to ignore it, think clearly
of Nadia's theme
and the pines of Minnesota.

He remembered
the white on white of a rabbit's
tracks in the snow,
white sun over Inchon,
those bugles, those faces; how
he survived and came home
to a life at Sikorsky, a warm
little kitchen with the souvenir
plates on the walls, ecology boxes
filled with grain and dried flowers,
telephone ringing, geese
flying across the cupboards.

I could have died for this, he thought,
and consciously turned
to the hand outside the window, stared
at it until it turned to icicles.

THE PERSISTENCE

All the children who were poets
have grown up now,
and up and down the street
they are fixing their houses.

A woman walks her German Shepherd
into the evening;
as if his life depended on it,
a man mows his lawn.

America's great sea of cars
has broken apart,
and come to rest in driveways,
by closed morning glories.

"Why me? And why my life?"
the television asks
a family being assembled
on the living room couch.

Bewildered, the woman goes
back to the kitchen;
under a faucet, she holds
a glass filled with water.

Over and over, she fills it
up to the brim
until she stares at it, pleased
nothing has happened.

Nothing has happened. The crickets
only come out,
the wind only blows. Life only
isn't, then is.

No, that's not right, she thinks,
and remembers a poem
by Kipling—or was it Yeats
who once broke her heart?

Under the hedges, the poets
lie on their backs;
smiling and singing together,
they bring forth the stars.

THE SPACESHIP ON ITS GANTRY

is
instantly primitive
as if the Earth had never existed
without the means for getting off it;
somehow, even on the planet, drawing
the darkness of space down around its long
nosed bullet grown enormous bulk, still strapped
in the orange girders of the gantry, lines
feeding it liquid oxygen, a beehive of men
around it as in the Brughel painting of the tower of Babel,
men climbing ladders, elevators moving up and down,
almost stroking its gun-metal sides; not yet
trembling, this the night before the night before the launch,
and the flats for miles around devoid of life except
for nightbirds roosting and the conical sunken shapes
of abandoned control centers, their innards ripped out,
grandstands covered with moss and always the oceans
out there, one seeming to be flat, the other curved
and waiting. The Moon. Venus. Mars. Jupiter. The nearest
galaxy. Quasars. Black holes. Star clusters. Constellations—
all out there, the little planet Earth way off in its
corner of the Milky Way. Why do I dream of it as often as
I dream of a woman's head in sunlight? Of it always at night, myself
standing before the Spaceship, orange flames spreading around its
    base
and then of the cities flattening out, the lakes becoming ponds,
becoming puddles, becoming nothing, covered by the clouds, the
    Earth
receding, dropping away like a penny—its copper rusted green—
I once threw out of the open cockpit of a piper cub I flew above
the small town in the Adirondack Mountains where I was raised
to believe in the Future through my science fiction paperbacks:
the great space poet Rhysling. Weinbaum's starry men, Hugo's
    creations,

Simak's cosmic engineers, Asimov's epic dreaming,
Stapledon's wonder and his tragedies. I remember how I once
argued with Lennie Brown that satellites *could* stay up
to circle the Earth, and lost that argument, and then the words
of Kennedy and his promise. And the night I woke my son
to watch Neil Armstrong step upon the moon; the dockings in space;
in a museum, a moonrock bathed in bluest light...so much
I seem to forget. Here, on Cocoa Beach, no crowds, the waves
from the Atlantic crashing as I walk and slap at mosquitoes
I think of it never existing, but it had to, just as the jungle
had to, the winds rise from the sea and blow us into clouds.

WALKING ACROSS THE LAKE

My father points down. There
is a 10-inch rainbow trout
completely frozen in the clear blue ice.
It is an Adirondack morning,
light snow drifting. Skaters
with hands behind backs, the unbearded
faces of the late 1940's,
loop, and taunt us as we walk. In Spring,
my father says, the ice
will melt, the trout will slide free, swim
to Kaydeross inlet. Still,
I don't like it. That night I'll wake
thinking the dark shape,
one eye looking up.

                    We walk
hours, over lily pads, a waterlogged oar,
broken cattails,
my father mostly quiet, only toward noon
consenting to pull me on the small blue sleigh
I am dragging. I lie
backwards, stomach down, head
almost touching the ice,
looking for a fish to swim away,
my father in some other thought of his.

AUTUMN LIGHTNING

Awakened by its flash, I count the seconds
with thousands, until the thunder booms
far to the east. I roll on my side,
pushing the red drapes from the windowsill
and think of how my grandmother always said
angels were falling. I picture them
crashing through the air, their stunning wings
heavy at their sides, their faces ashen
as they plummet. Another strike, another
and my wife wakes up in the darkness,
clutching the bedclothes to her breasts.
"Angels are falling," I whisper
as we listen to the rain whip into froth
against the new siding. Now they are overhead
seeking the mirrors, the scissors; now
they fly through the room, driven, driven
to find us in panic. Whole constellations
burn in their robes; haloes ignite,
hair floats around their shoulders. My wife
stares at the clock and trembles
until the storm passes into distant numbers.
Earth is the same,
oaks being shriven, maples touched by their fire.

TO AN ASTRONAUT VISITING A JAPANESE GARDEN AT NIGHT

Those few branches reaching for the moon
    out of all these trees, out of all this forest,
if they were carved upon a vase on some museum table,
    the moon falling among them, and the vase was green,
would take you back up through the stars, despite
    the interventions of a world you knew by hand.

A WINTER MORNING

All night I thought of Leningrad, the streetlights
    blinking in the snow, the women's faces
staring out from high apartment windows,
    and the trees bent down with snow, the disappearance
of the husbands, their returnings, how
    women's faces are like candle flames.

How cold it was! I thought of wooden drays
    pulled by horses, and a driver's hands
pulled into sleeves, false dawn, the gray
    long boulevard between the blocks of houses
looming over him; how his face betrays
    not a single thought that is not his.

Snow falling into snow, a mongrel scampering
    back and forth across the boulevard,
a doorway lighted for a moment, vanishing
    as the door is closed, an old
man keeps walking up and down; he keeps on brushing
    snow from off his overcoat and beard.

I thought of all the cherished and uncherished lives
    that vanish from each other, how sometimes
we start toward strangers and they turn away, their eyes
    downcast, remembering the bends
of rivers under ice, how the wind will slide
    all living creatures down the glossy slopes.

And you from me, sometime. And you from me.
    Ground cover me, and wind your ashes take;
our stories, stories; and our headlong dreams
    spun into other dreams, or tiny breaks
between the clouds. What we tried to mean
    is not what we became or could forsake.

The snow fell harder; soon the street became
    a swirling tunnel filled with voices as
awed children yelled from stoops, and names
    turned oddly into syllables, the trees
bent against the hedges and the windows slammed
    deeper into ice-glazed windowsills.

I heard you call me by a name not mine,
    but somehow fitting. There was tea
warmed beside the pilot light. Your face was framed
    in soft and loosened hair; the tapestry
of morning love was in your touch, a line
    of snow fell curving from the balcony.

LETTER FROM THE COLONIES

Two days into this region and already I
have trouble with sleep....
The winds blow nightly.... It is exhausting
to keep writing down
descriptions of fine full trees, the bushy animals,
herbs such as I had never thought to stoop and touch
and how this river flows, the banks of this river,
gorges, waterfalls, glades, even the rain
comes down I think wrongly.... It reminds me of
cross-hatching, as it seems to slant
back and forth across a mountain or a valley,
caving one part in and bringing one to light
and I am tired but elated.... Too much
wonder, too much awe.... It is not England,
not safe like England.... Raw, wild, wilderness
such as would make you gasp. Passions
I would you never suffer
(though I remember how the strength of you
surprised, embarrassed, on that first dark night
in the bed, your body unclothed!) have their grasp
upon us all, I think.... It is the Autumn
of this unstructured world. Leaves have blown away
from whole mountainsides.... Clinging
to rocks and the unclothed branches I have pulled
myself to such heights.... I have stood before
such vistas, I fear I shall never
again be sensible to small
delights, the pleasures of quiet piano.
Yet I miss
you, I miss you. By the firelight, writing
you this letter,
I can see my hands tremble, you observe
even the slant of my words upon this paper
has changed.... Were you here

we should be resting sweetly in some pine
bower and your limbs would once again
so delight me that I should not speak.... My love,
I thrill to the word *America* as I
thrilled to find you so uncalm.... Tomorrow
more walking.... We are all transformed,
the very least of us, the stupid boy,
the dumbest of my men.... They hang
upon my words, they are desperate for words,
something to make this all seem civilized, a first
taming, to tell them what
they are seeing, they are feeling.... Never have
I felt this power, this duty
to record.... We have lain down
beside a broad lake where the deer
step into the water, unafraid. Great flocks
of geese are upon it also....
Only once before
have I so felt I lived,
breathing with your body heaved to mine.

THE PEOPLE THROUGH THE TRAIN WINDOW

All we'll ever know of them are the lights
of their houses in the late evening winter,
and that their lives are intertwined as ours,
as lonely as a Scott Fitzgerald story.

Born to rush out on the earth and die,
how strangely we behave, as if it were not true
that there will be old gravestones up above our bodies,
and our children will be thinking of us sometime.

How else can I say it? We will die
and not come back, not ever, not return
to mystic restaurants and words we've spoken softly,
stroking, glances, and confessions, and

the seasons of this lovely planet will take no
notice of our vanishing; my hands
will lie as silently as yours; the wind
above the planet will not touch your eyes,

nor, within a hundred years, one face
of those within the houses with the lighted rooms.
Can we imagine that? All dead, all dead,
all of us all dead, who never lived enough.

Good Lord, the carpe diem poets in their graves
were so right that it makes me tremble when
I think of falling into love, and out, and in again,
or listen to Jim Croce in his Creole voice.

Seize the day, oh seize the day, oh seize
your life with every tendon, every thought you have;
the moonlight hits the window, and the stars
have always gone this crazy in their crazy sky.

SMALL HOTEL

When you open the window on the balcony
    and the English sparrows stay there on the railing
above the small garden, expecting to be fed
    or at least not shooed away—still in your nightclothes,
you feel it improper not to stretch your arms
    wide and think of angels visiting the Earth
on a morning like this, for no special reason
    except to once again experience a place
of small rooms, small beds, small hallways and the hopes
    gratefully diminished, without a sense of mission
or thundering glory. Beyond the garden wall
    and wishing well with its carpet of old pennies,
the streets are cobblestoned; mop-haired children roll
    hoops to the parish school. The first loud-voiced
vendor makes his rounds and one by one
    cottage windows open, heads of old women
pop into the sunshine. If you were a painter,
    you would be Dutch and lovingly would enter
kitchens for the sake of wooden cupboards,
    fruit on the tables, knives with thick handles
crosswise in the plumpest loaves of bread. What you
    would do with that bread! How many mornings
you've risen in your own house with no view
    except to what's expected, felt no sense of all
the unexpected, ordinary miracles of light and sound
    strange rooms, strange countries and strange lives reveal
on the first morning. Behind you, in the unmade bed,
    the one you love is shaking loose her hair
and wondering about the weather. Fine!
    Fantastic! Marvelous! you want to shout. The air
is cool yet briefly touched with pools of warmth
    as in a spring-fed lake before the season starts
for ordinary swimming and you're swimming anyway,
    constantly surprised, unable to make sense

or pattern from such wells of water trapped
   in wider spells of water. Steeple bells
start ringing through the valleys. When you dress—
   when you descend beside the wooden bannisters
to breakfast, burghers with their florid faces touched
   by beams of sunlight will be sitting in the cleared
nook off the kitchen. Everything will shine, will be
   without such anguish it is possible to say
with all true meaning in the language of the bursting heart,
   good morning, good, good morning, Christ it's good
each moment to each moment in this small hotel,
   this place on Earth with windows and the garden,
and the tulips gathering and bursting by the wall.

MIDLIFE

What is worse than feeling your smile go awful
minutes before you are to meet the person
you supposedly love, worse even than waking up
from a dream of a stranger, with her arms
or his arms wrapped about you and you must
say something into those fawning eyes that won't
hurt, and yet won't be a lie—what is worse
is the first time you cannot do it, cannot bring
the smile back in time, or when the words
will not rise to the surface and you helplessly
are silent, unable to prevent
everything going wrong because you want it to.

THE AFTERLIFE

At the end of our journey, which we took
only half-knowing it would bring us here
to this place of savage red blossoms
and rivers quietly swaying through the rocks,
this place of taut winds,
night longer than a monk's long prayer,
we found each other, and we recognized
each other, and your hands were still
warm from their living. I could almost see
the blood flow back to your lips, your eyes
begin to return
from that impossible darkness. "Did
our love survive?" I asked.
"I don't know," you answered, and then paused,
came further back, and nodded. "Yes,
yes, yes, it did."
               And now we've built
a small wood cabin in whatever place
this is.
We've learned to talk again, not of
the past, we don't remember well, but how
quiet are the meadows, and the strange
beautiful birds
that we've begun to name, the hush
at nightfall when a calmness seems to slip
about this world
and something is so right, you cry,
holding me, and listen for the footfall that
we are certain will come.
And in the mornings, when I see your face,
your naked body graceful as you walk
beside me to the spring,
in your off-center voice, you sing
so awkwardly, so happily, I seem

for a moment to recall where we once were,
some place of green and blue, some old
city where we drank red wine
and strangers thought us lovers as we laughed
about your sense of time,
the buildings falling upwards through the sky.

CROSSING THE STARS ON NEW YEAR'S EVE

Another year. As if exercising its right to be a symbol,
the digital clock breaks down at 12:15
with a sound like birds chirping. I open the drapes
and stare at the empty house across the woodlot,
beyond it Thrushwood Lake—an old-fashioned oval mirror
fallen in snow, reflecting the moonlight.

Such moonlight! It is as if I'm staring
into a winter batik, cracked with the lines
of birches and poplars—or a jigsaw puzzle
glued together, hung on a flickering wall
beneath a spotlight shining from the ceiling,
the light between the lines absorbed, absorbing.

Behind me, in your long blue gown, you're watching
a movie of the Alps. The mountain climbers each
have sown a shriveled eagle's tongue inside their coats;
and one is snow-blind, holding up the rest.
You whisper, "Look at this." I turn and he is falling,
tumbling, bouncing, sliding from the crest.

I shiver, thinking of a face inside a cowl,
how too great clarity makes things untrue,
and it starts snowing now. The oval lake turns white,
a backdrop for an onyx cameo.
Nothing in a film, say cameramen, is quite so beautiful
as scenes shot through the slowly falling snow.

You shut the television off. A blanket wrapped around
your shoulders, you stand by me. All out there
is fading into white. The hills, the lake, the house,
the woodlot—all are gone. The moon has disappeared
inside a bank of clouds. Just swirling snow
I shine a flashlight into meets our eyes.

"But how beautiful," you say, "a tunnel, look!"
And we peer into it, along the flashlight's beam,
at crystals spiraling. It's as if we've poked
a hole right through a swirling galaxy
of dense stars. At the tunnel's end
a living tree stands branched out like a man.

OVERNIGHT IN THE GUEST HOUSE
OF THE MYSTIC

I

Here, in a small house with no telephone,
my brother-in-law
leaps against a board, and snarls, and kicks it through,
then bows to his Master—
a look-alike for Tung-fang So—that rascal
who stole the Peaches of Longevity.

At night, the wind
whistles through the halyards of the pleasure boats
down in the bay;
a teenage car
screeches through the turns down Flower Hill,
then all is still.

Visiting, I lie awake and think
how strangely we have reached the huge world state
where "east meets west" is more than just a phrase
from Kipling's poem
and raindrops in the gutters sound
like water dripping on a bamboo drum.

If I could live so long, if I could ride
Night-shining White
through the luminosity of days
breaking endlessly, beside persimmon trees,
or through the English forests, or above
the coves of France—would I take that chance?

Would I steal the Peaches of Longevity
and eat them by myself? I dream
of histories ahead, the quasars flowering
upon the edge of space; odd specks of light

like fireflies in the pines, the first
new cities of another galaxy.

Which marks me of my time—which turns
almost helplessly between
huge shadows and the drifting stars,
a boat upon a boat at sea
floating in a bottle, each uplifted sail
raised to catch a wind that cannot be.

II

In Chinese parks
long lines of workers stand out in the dawn,
slow motion dancing by themselves.
Impossible to say what they are thinking
removed into the dance, the dance
removing all the gestures of their lives.

So many, many lives! I give
up counting them. A seaplane makes its way
up the Carolina coast. Beneath the red
and blue lights of its wings, the bulk
of its fuselage,
people in there, too. More lives, more lives.

Sometimes, I am aware no matter how
I plan, consult the waterways
and large outstanding books, breathe in and out,
each moment is an accident, a nudge
of one thing toward another, energy
exploding into matter ceaselessly.

We sat around the fireplace. David spoke
of standing on a fence and looking out
across the plains of Illinois, until he thought
he saw an eagle hovering above
a farmhouse chimney's tiny line of smoke,
his motorcycle fallen in a cloud of dust.

The mystic's consciousness. It heightens and
diminishes our lives. The German tanks
move against the sabres of the Poles.
A man displays
a little courage and he dies. The autumn grass
sways above his body, bends and sways.

III

Peach juice dribbles down my chin. I am
a satyr dancing in the olive grove,
my wife a naked maiden. In the pool
among the women washing out their hair,
their wrists and ankles in the lily pads,
I spring; I take her there.

The willing violence of the ways we fling
our bodies toward each other is my answering
to all that fills the cracks with mold and dust,
tarnishes, and turns the streams to rust
beneath the maples swaying on an autumn day.
But, in rough translation, David's masters say:

Turn back the steed, replace the peach, attempt
to reach that place

where knowledge turns to wisdom, as a light green wash
of paint upon a pair of screens might turn
into a crane, a crescent moon, a morning glory
or Kōrin's bamboo forests by a lonely lake.

Live to praise
your being mystified, the accidental glimpse
of doors through doorways, flames inside the flames,
groundless triumphs and the wind
whistling through the halyards of Port Washington;
the touch of hands.

Make light of darkness; make of darkness light
as John Martin did, who cast upon
his canvas so much glory, even in
the drowning rush a hand reached out, a wrist
was grasped and all the angels sang
in unison to see the boundless Lord.

IV

Ten years ago, within a dream he'd died,
two lovely women, strangers to his eyes,
took David's arms and led him to the chairs
beside an empty fireplace where they sat and talked.
The cottage had plank floors. There was
a casement window open to his left.

He rose and walked to it, and looking out
saw a meadow filled with light; the grasses came
almost to his hands upon the windowsill
as he bent over it. He felt

ecstatic, without memory, and then
he woke, remembered everything.

V

Headlights from the passing cars
make streaks across the walls. A silk Nō robe
hangs against the door; outside the room
his two dogs pace and settle, whine
a little when they hear a jet
pass overhead.

He's happy. Does it all come down to that?
Both search and meditation leading to
acceptance, but on different planes
between the worlds continuous—as long as we
break through
and see into the lands beyond ourselves?

Our task is to acknowledge how the moths
dance upon a hayfield, darkling speed
of bats in flight above the ocean's spume;
give thanks, his masters say, for all
that takes our breath away and makes us see
more clearly through Illusion's fading veils.

Our knowledge that we shall not pass this way again—
almost unbearable—although it makes
each moment precious in itself,
strikes even deeper if we come to feel
the signs and patterns of the mystical
on every tree and bush and turning wheel.

VI

The *feng-huang*, when it flies, attended by
The Hundred Birds,
will not harm a living thing, appears
only in the country when the clear
times of reason have prevailed, and otherwise
hides itself beside the peony.

I long to see it fly again. I picture it
not in this roundel high on David's wall,
but soaring through the heavens at the break
of dawn upon Long Island Sound, and hear
its mystic voice
sing beautifully above a hundred bells.

I light the table lamp. The lacquer box
containing brushes, inkstone, ink, a water dropper,
sits upon the nightstand. To the black slate well
I've watched him pour the water, take the ink stick, dip
and scrape against the surface of the stone,
and on a fine scrolled paper, paint the words.

First he describes
the cherry tree that leans above the torrent.
Then the rush of water through the rocks
and then another tree, its branches in those clouds
carved in gold against a brilliant black
so deep it overwhelms the scene it holds.

Through the hours left of night
and into morning when the first child rolls

beneath his window, on a skate board, laughing merrily,
he writes. And then he swims
out by Gatsby's Point, where butterflies,
he's told me, dance for ages on the wind.

VII

Lamp dark again,
I settle into sleep between my old
boundaries of right and wrong. Tomorrow,
not that I've understood, but that I've sensed
limits may be bridged, not gone against,
shall I walk calmer through my changing world?

Although I'm neither strong nor weak enough
to give up anguish yet, nor set aside
my outrage toward the things I cannot change
which make us into slaves or animals
with neither choice nor consciousness of choice,
these might be just Illusions like the rest.

Still, passion overwhelms me, is not tamed. I've felt
love burst within me like a hundred stars.
Should I lose all this?
The Way lies just before me, an unopened gift
forever possible. For now, is it enough
to touch the paper wrapping of a thousand cranes?

Through David's tiny garden, stepping quietly
among the bonsai trees and stream-washed stones
creeps Tung-fang So,

his ankles tangled in his robes,
a withered hand outstretched to steal the peach
higher up the trunk than his poor eyes can reach.

There is a city there, out in the mist. The boats
surround it on three sides, and from
the other side, behind the castle walls
a stretch of mossy ground leads far beyond
to somewhere David saw, or seemed to—an impossible
yet possible existence. Much, I think, like ours.

UNIVERSITY STUDENTS
STROLLING THROUGH MIDNIGHT

for Robert Ira Karmon

I think of the night we walked through Syracuse,
that park with yellow moths around its streetlights.
We were two young men, dreaming of being famous.
The last trains from Rochester and Utica
slowed into the station on Erie Boulevard—
lines of typewriters clicking in the distance.
Above the old city a gibbous moon hung tiredly,
casting shadows through the pines, along the paths.
The spring wind at our backs was the pressure
of jackets grown too tight across the shoulders.
We talked, as young men talk, of many books
we read as if we were wading a stream in a clearing;
in words to our knees, we balanced in the currents.
Such nights, I am convinced, occur but once
between two friends, before they part with a handshake.
Restaurants closed, we shared that special licorice
you always carried—as we paused in the moonlight
beside the tennis courts and you told your stories
of growing up in the Catskills, your twin brother
pulled out dead a few minutes before you were born.
I spoke of the Adirondacks, where my uncle
built a log road skirting a huge white lake.
Under the streetlights, the moths became our stories
corkscrewing up to the lamps and falling away.
Where we would live! Providence and Dayton,
Philadelphia, New York, Westport, Garden City.
We sought a fame that would never grow as large
as we vowed it would; we live still with our wives;
we raise our children: your daughters, my son and daughter.
You said the moths were dreams among the branches
under the streetlights, that they would vanish.
But you were wrong, for I see them now—
each bite of wings, each spiral, each mad dashing.

I see you raise your head to them, my eyes
following your gestures and I hear the typewriter trains:
their fading messages, the hands above them lifted.
I feel the night wind and the moon descending;
the sky is a curious black and gray without ending.
Its surface is cracked but holding like the glaze
of a painting, or a bowl from the Corning kilns.
The flowers by the paths are wings of scattered moths.

SUNSHOWER

At the end of a dream, where there are exit signs
leading to morning
and figures squatting in the dust
casting *I Ching,*
you try to remember
the kiss on your lips, dried flowers in the sun,
a red and silver box of Chinese coins,
the dictionary picture of umbrella birds
above the green forest. Campfires dot the roads,
and meadows appear. A tiny pontoon plane
is flying just above the clouds. You start to walk,
arms swinging, toward a cottage that
might have been Wordsworth's—with the old stone barn
beside it, chimney shaped
like the top of a lighthouse. Back, come back, you hear
faint voices calling.
               The road
you've chosen is all overhung
with nodding leaves and branches and it curves
before you're ready, opening upon
green pastures where some horses graze,
their heads uplifted as you pause again,
make light of them,
and wake up with the sun against your face.
               A window near
the bedside's open and the screen
is pattered like the game of *Go*—a hundred beads
of water clinging to it just before
they're flung against you. Looking out, you see
the world has changed
to fluid streaks of light, lines crossing lines,
and raindrops blinking everywhere they fall.

MYSTICAL LEANINGS

Don't take this lightly—how the forest burns
out of control along a ridge of pines
and the clouds look like warships. Everything reveals
the presence of something else to live with under heaven:
pulled over meadows, the taut ropes of Autumn,
asteroids, moon. A horse is whinnying
as he gallops down a blacktop road. In open car windows
heads can be seen. Your own face is a sheet
of white ice to the passing cars. Behind you, land
stretches beneath the trees. Why can't you hold
the presence of this, bathe in the sun, swim your way across
each day as if it were the last—not live
in a mansion of pictures? Eckhart once saw
a flock of crows above him as he walked,
that flew out of his mind. You've been to the desert
at a monastery made from wood, where no one talked
to the silent monks in the courtyard, shapes
without voices, the living imitations
of bird and beast and fowl before the light;
and deeply in love
as any man or woman capsized in a storm,
you heard the nightingale sing sweetly through
bare English woods—the night you returned
from the edge of Korea. Say it over softly, softly, how
there aren't any words, only expressions, only
hills leading to valleys. Maya, Maya, Maya—
chants and shadows taking place by fire;
and count up to ten. There's no protection
from what your eyes can't see, your mind can't comprehend,
but prayer and vision and the real horse galloping
along the blacktop road, sound of his hooves
slowly fading backward as if listening.

GREEN PASTURES

The boy who has crawled
through the barbed wire fence to chase his dog
lies down in green pastures. Off to the right
a cottage and an old stone barn
look serenely deserted. Is there a soul
that cannot be restored? A time on the planet
all bets are called off? I have seen such pastures
at the end of Korea, littered with bodies, the medics
fanning across them like a flock of butterflies
to opening flowers. There is a pasture
high in the Adirondacks Winslow Homer painted
with two stabs of light. The boy seems asleep
or trying to close his eyes so tightly he will enter
the mind of his dog. All bets off? What does it take
to convince you that the hills are not asleep,
and the boy is not dreaming? Turning back and forth
in a North Dakota pasture is a radar screen
looking out for the Russians. In a small bowl of hills
wires are strung above deep pasture grass
to catch the faintest traffic from the stars
parsecs away. It is hopeless
to ignore a world that did not pass away
despite our avowals. Sunrise. Sunset. The green
stems of grass that touch against the boy
seem to hold the wind in place. A tractor
ridden by the brushstroke of a man
has been weaving for hours
on the farmlands behind us. Surely it is time
to rest, to lie down in the green beneath the blue
and call it a day
or if we cannot do that, call it something given
to us—like sleep and waking up and sometimes rain
standing in the air around us as we walk
gratefully through it and it parts a little while.

FROM
FLIGHT AND PURSUIT

CITIES & EMPIRES

The secret is not to move, the lady said,
But sometimes you can turn your head away
For a minute, then back, as you do to really watch
A sunset, and you do this several times, and then
You can feel the dark on your eyes like a cold cloth.

That's how it was, she said. When the soldiers went by—
straight lines of them, like holes in a cribbage board;
Men no older than my boy they caused to vanish—
I stood, but stared at nothing. Others told me
A haze of apple petals fell about them slowly.

And when I looked back, they were gone. The road
Was empty, save for cars with blackened seats,
And a body or two. It was comforting, that quiet,
For I was thinking of coffee, I was thinking
Of holding my hands around a cup of coffee.

You must do it, after all, she said—your eating,
Washing, sleeping, suffering. The mind has little rooms
It rents out to the body, and at times
You go there, no one follows you, the shades are drawn,
Dust falls like fingers from each one you touch.

NOTES AFTER ETHER

I'd wanted to bring back something from that darkness:
A spool, a few star flecks, a water lily...
But when I woke, I could remember only
The nurses' hands that held mine as I counted
Upwards and never reached ten, the doctor's face
Blurring into the ceiling as he disappeared.

Wheeled back to my room, I spent an hour watching
It rain into Bridgeport, how the rainfall kept
The streets, the porches of the tenements
Below my window deserted. I remember
A broken box kite dangling from a string
Caught on a power line...the O's of abandoned tires.

There had to be something. I closed my eyes and searched
Back into the darkness, as one does
When woken from dead sleep, looking for a cause
Of sweat on the temple, hands held stiffly outright,
Ready for a reencounter on whatever road
Went curving through the sycamores at midnight.

Yet, nothing. Under my left leg's bandages, the blood
Clotted, staining brown. The rental TV
Above my head, locked in its swivel assembly,
Offered the world through a simple set of knobs
I'd twist when I was ready. Now I was tired
And wanted none of it. My left leg throbbed,

My roommate lay drugged. Against the small window
Steadily rattling in its thin aluminum frame,
Cellophane rain gusts came and went and came,
Blurring and clearing and blurring the draggled city
When Barnum once put elephants on show:
"If it doesn't play in Bridgeport, it won't play."

110

Then, one by one, my visitors pushed through the door:
Family, friends. In the softened crevices
Of their rain clothes, in their folded umbrellas
And finger-combed hair, scores of raindrops sparkled,
Catching fluorescent light. What more, what more
Had I ever wanted, should I have expected?

When they'd left, nurses' hands shooing them out,
A residue of books and rainy flowers
Lay scattered around my room. A bunch of doctors
From India came to inspect me—in their singing English
Pronouncing me salvaged, almost beyond doubt;
Smiled and nodded, and very shortly vanished.

My roommate gone, wheeled to his own operation,
I lay in the room alone. The rainfall slackened;
Houselights, streetlights, carlights—all that happened
To the world outside me patterning the glass
As Bridgeport fell away. I turned the television on.
I let the swarthy heroes have the darkness.

GRANDFATHER'S JIGSAW PUZZLE

As you work with the faded pieces,
A man's head over here, the blue of the ocean
And sky still confused,
A huge elm growing by itself
Off in the corner,
You think of the world's old mistress, the moon
Looking in the window of a 19th-century poem,
And the summer patio
Where even the conversations about change
Don't change. You think of how many meanings
Drift into nothing, sure answers
Come to be disproved. Slowly, you form
A woman's body curving in a hammock,
The house in the distance,
And wonder why you seem about to weep
As the pieces get closer, bridges
Appear between the sections and dissolve
Into parts of the landscape;
And it is determined
That what you took to be a solid man
Was his broken reflection
Floating in a small pool by the garden's edge,
And the picture was something else
You had not dreamed of:
A landscape of a cottage by the sea
As evening was coming
So naturally it took you by surprise;
And the eastern barred owl
Nesting in the elm tree, fifty feet up,
Not minding how you worked your life away.

IF YOU VISIT OUR COUNTRY

At night, in the little towns that crop up in America
Where the highway curves beside a riverbank
Or lifts you suddenly up a drumlin to the lights
Left burning in closed restaurants and filling stations,
Someone is always walking with a dog, and someone
Is always standing at a window looking pensive.

And if you drive on further through the pensive
Fields and leaning forests of America,
Singing or dreaming, and you share the wheel with someone
You love, you will likely see a bank
Of stars in the west. Tune to an all-nite station
Playing crazy rock. The world will be blinking lights

Racing toward you or away, your headlights
Picking up old things along the highway: pensive
And dilapidated barns, abandoned railroad stations,
The culverts, junkyards, flagpoles of America
That never left the Thirties—the small-town bank
Closed for the Depression, then reopened. Someone

Is always starting out or starting over; someone
In jeans and open shirt has seen her name in lights
Or told a cowlicked boyfriend he can bank
Upon the future. In every town a pensive
Father reminisces to his son about America,
Or a priest is walking slowly through the Stations

Of the Cross, praying he might rise above his station
In this anguished life, becoming someone
Truly worthy, truly, truly worthy. All across America
You will find embracing lovers under streetlights,
Tiger lilies, Queen Anne's lace, the pensive
Look of high schools closed for summer, empty banks

Of bleacher seats at baseball games; and if you bank
Hard where the highway curves, and if you station
Yourself securely at the wheel, sooner or later pensive
Thoughts will overcome you. Try to be someone
For whom the country opens, for whom traffic lights
At empty crossroads signify America:

The shades and awnings of America, the kid who banks
A billiard shot, fizzed neon lights, the military station
High on Someone's Bluff, the sentry walking pensive.

WILLIAM RIMMER: FLIGHT AND PURSUIT

I saw two men in flight and in pursuit,
Stone castle walls around them and their bodies bent
As if they were the same. They were not the same
But in the leaning shadows of my dream
First I wore a dagger and a sash—
I fled the Lord's white lash;
Then a curving sword, a hood across my face—
I sped through darkness on His headlong chase.

I could not gain; I could not lose. We stayed
Near, not closing nearer. I could hear the wind
Roaring through the turrets, fleshing out the flags;
Beggars' hands reached up from beggars' rags,
Doorways turned to rooms; we sped through rooms
To other doorways—eyes, hands, bare thighs numb
As gods in bas-relief. The rooms went on and on;
Neither of us stumbled as we ran.

My mind, like all minds, sought a single room without
Another doorway; or, another world beyond it.
In either place I could have turned and drawn
My dagger from my sash; I could have shown
The face beneath this hood. But as we passed
Each portal, sandals burning, thinking it the last,
One more, one more. His sandals raced before
And followed me across each stone slab floor.

THE COMMUTER

On the Triborough Bridge, thinking of galaxies,
How Herschel said they strayed like garden beds
Seeding, blooming, fading, withering
Before his eyes as he stared back through Time,
I inch along in a cluster of April night
Traffic going home. Off to all sides,
The city's constellations: *Rachel's Dress,*
The Wineglass, The Cathedral Radio, Joe's Hat,
The Wad of Money, Whitman's Yawp, Crane's Leap
In storefront patterns and apartment lights.
Guarding the exit ramp, a girl with freckled hands
Holds yellow roses to each passing car.
I buy a dozen. Flung to the empty seat,
They toss and bend beside me down one spiral arm.

THE PHYSICIST TO HIS LOST LOVE

Last summer is months away and still the cicadas
Have not finished their stories. They keep telling them
As if they were responsible for every background
You keep stepping from. Some nights I dream we're standing
Under a streetlight, unable to touch;
Their familiar drone becomes so overwhelming
It almost seems we're sinking into their drab music
And soon will be only phosphors on a TV screen.

If worlds lie parallel, like rings around a barrel,
And if there is another me, another you close by
Or somewhere further back or further on,
Are we this intense, or less? How much
Can love diverge? In alternating worlds, do you still hold
Your hand up to your lips when frightened,
Pore over maps to find the hidden streams,
And read yourself to sleep with Henry James?

Or did you come from one of them, and have returned,
Leaving in your place a twin or clone
Who shares your memory but lacks the chromosome
Which held your disposition to be close to me?
"Der Herrgott würfelt nicht," and yet He may
With a sense of humor or despair. Immense beliefs
Topple from their own immensity;
We ride the waves to random eigenstates

As thought rides thought in search of certainty,
Or raindrops ride the branches of a withered tree.
Forgive. I'm so caught up in bubble chambers,
And studying the pathways of decaying particles
To check the probable, the language of the lab
Is a birth caul on the face of what I mean to say

About our love. Yet, I can't break free
To say it openly. Mock me if you must

But let my language try for its own dignity
However awkward is the merging of the scientific
With those splendid intuitions from your literature
By novelists and poets. Schrödinger's cat
May be living or sprawl dead. It may be the act
Of looking that decides. We have to look
And take our chances. All the universe I understand
Or seem to understand has been enraptured

With our observations. Last summer, when we walked
Across that meadow where the goldenrod
And Queen Anne's lace and black-eyed Susans poked
Every here and there above the swaying bunchgrass
You said our love was certain and would last,
But my mind turned upon itself and found no truth,
Although, God knows, I loved you. In my silence
Did the wave collapse or ripple when cicadas droned?

THE SWING

When I let go
    And way up there
Sat for a moment
    On thin air,

Feet dangling, hands
    Still shoulder-high,
I didn't hear
    Mother's cry

But only thought
    She'll love to see
Her offspring flying
    Crazily

Above her friends
    Across the yard;
I guess that's why she
    Pushed so hard.

EVENING TRAIN (1949)

Where the D&H from Albany to Montreal
Curved in snowy woods beyond our town
We would kneel by creosote ties—and, bending down,
Place our ears to the rails.

Miles back, we could hear it: the 7:15
Cutting through pines, running on time,
Approaching the trestle high above Route 9
In a sound like wind makes in a small ravine.

And because we'd long practiced
Hearing the future, we knew when it slowed
At the D&H station, mailbags thrown to the road,
And then picked up speed—at the first

Straight stretch past the Lutheran church
Smashing into the woods. Even gripped tight,
Our hands couldn't feel it. Yet at the instant
Small bones in our ears began to lurch

We threw our bodies away, we rolled
Gasping and laughing down the steep embankment
Of weeds and snow and gravel and cement,
There to lie on our backs—and behold

The great beam of light. It split the pines,
It split our voices and it split our lives
Like they were nothing. The ties
Shook as it passed. Silent, we regained the lines

And balancing, balancing, foot after foot,
Tried to tightrope them home.
The loser was who fell off first. I remember the boom
Of ice on Jones' Pond: a boxcar door being shut.

CROWS AND WINDMILLS

Crows and windmills—sounds of American farmland
When the sky is overcast and the wind blows at evening.

As someone like Burchfield would know, taking down his easel
In the Depression, and starting the long stroll back

Through a meadow of swaying bunchgrass to the county road
Where his running-board Ford is waiting tiredly

Pulled to the side, and gray as weathered clapboard
Of houses that seem to exist only in distance.

Tonight, I heard them again, but it was in a movie
And only for some minutes while a girl in overalls

Walked with her head down from her drunken father
Toward a hill and a tree like a clawed hand toppling over

Against the October sky. I shivered. The windmill's blades
Blurred in a wooden cluttering; the crows made dives

Toward the open silo, cawing and cawing with that
Raw scratch of the throat that makes me think *O Sinner-Man,*

Where you gonna run to? Such heavy loneliness
Came over me I had to grip the next row's empty seatback

Until the scene was done. I had been returned
To Roark's farm, and had heard a third sound: the dry

Snap and whisper of thousands of rows of cornstalks
A gang of us were playing in, losing ourselves on purpose,

Then leaping high as we could to see above them, calling
Our names out: A parody of what would become our lives,

Moon bleeding, stars falling, sea sinking, rocks rolling
All on that day. As a joke, my friends snuck off, and I

Was left leaping and calling to no one when the dusk
Came on. Desperate, I leaped and called and leaped and called

Among the cornstalks until, exhausted, I fell
And rolled over, panting; in the overcast, I saw

A flock of crows, the pattern so jagged it was almost vicious.
Each crow, as the flock passed above me, cawed out its warning

More to itself than others, and when, at last, I followed
The windmill sound, it became a huge gray daisy

Whirring above the barn.... Farmer Roark found me
And drove me home in a red truck splattered with rust

When I couldn't stop crying and shaking. My parents
Had not known I was gone, worked to the bone as they were.

NIGHT SLEDDING

From Lookout Hill it was a long way down to the village.
The plowed steep road no cars would dare until morning
And the pine trees snowed into each other, forming ruined
Castles and English manor houses and gamekeeper huts
In the ravines and gullies and stark on the ridges,
Seemed more ours than anything would ever be again,
Whether our lives were short or long. I glanced
At the others to see if they felt it: the loosened knot
Of boys whose fathers were mostly off in World War II,
Kneeling and panting in the snow, their bodies
Gnomed by bulky jackets, their faces small round windows
Sunk in wool, and saw their tremors
Of frozen-tongued awe, and how they tried to hide them
As I was trying, also, to not say anything
Too stupid or old. There were gusts of wind
Constantly sending clouds of powdered white
Off the rock outcroppings. Above us, a half-blasted moon
Was painted on a white sandpaper field of stars.

"Let's get going," someone said. Hand-me-down sleds
Lined up, lying on our bellies, boot tips dug into snowruts,
We studied the village below us, the far-off lights
Of the D&H station, the Methodist church steeple,
Lights in the upstairs windows of a dozen cottages
And "Isn't this something," the boy beside me whispered,
"Isn't this something!" Who started, I don't remember,
But suddenly, faces held up, yelling for dear life,
All of us yelling and whooping, we were steering
Our sleds in great S's as we fell,
None of us trying to win, all of us half-crazed, shouting,
"Watch out! Hang on! Steer to the side!
Steer to the middle! Drop behind! Go ahead!"
Sparks from rocks our runners scraped, and then
At the last sweet drop, an absolute silence among us

As we swooped down, and some of our mothers and sisters
Waiting beneath the streetlights, some applauding
With soft mittened claps as we slowed. Walking home,
My house the last one before the village became a meadow,
I saw a comet streak, leaving in its wake
A crowfoot of light, gone the moment I blinked.

CLAPPING ERASERS

Numbers and words go up in blue-white puffs
At the ends of my hands. Here, on the school's back porch,
I make the erasers do a Morse code SOS
Until, like minds at Recess, each is cleansed.

I can see Round Lake from here, and Lavery's pontoon planes;
One is revving up, about to take
The fast run toward the pines. It will almost skim them
On its way to Saratoga or Mechanicville.

At twelve, I'm caught in Time and loving it:
The unmown grass, the marble ring, the Ford
With running boards my father lets me stand on,
And my teachers, Mrs. Copins and Miss Turner

Who (and Lavery) will die throughout the Sixties.
But now they pass out Coca-Cola rulers
And teach us Tennyson and Browning, and despite ourselves
Machine-gun recitation of times tables.

I even have a paper route. Each morning
On my Shelby bike, I pedal through my village
And throw the news through railings, or tuck it inside doors.
It's all about the halves of Jell-O boxes,

Truman and MacArthur, and the Brooklyn Dodgers.
It's all about my life, but I don't know that yet.
Another city or another place on earth
Vanishes each time I clap erasers.

And one of Lavery's planes is coming down,
Circling, and then it hits the waves.
Its pontoons leave a wash like puffy railroad tracks
Into the lily pads where Mr. Lavery stands,

Flagging the pilot in. My arms are white and scratchy;
My face looks like a mime's. One more call for help
Before I'm done. When Miss Turner leans
Out of her window, I'll be her boy of dust.

THE WORKERS

I

They make their way up the hill in Burchfield's painting
So tiredly, so one by one, it is as if their bodies
Are still at the lathes. My father, like this, came home
Winters from the railway yards. Often he didn't talk
For hours as my brother and I played around him,
Climbing his belly, pretending he was dead
While he lay on the big flowered couch and watched our mother
Stand at her ironing board in the kitchen doorway
Or pass back and forth before him, hands in an apron
She even wore, sometimes, over her nightgown.

II

In another Burchfield painting, at six o'clock
I wait in a snowdrift near a row of houses
While my family has supper. Great long icicles
Hang from gray eaves and porches. The backdoor steps
Are shoveled only enough for a single person
To climb without slipping. Through curtainless windows
I see bare walls above the heads about the table,
Except for a shelf that holds the plain white pitcher
And bowl I will one day break. Two houses down,
Floating beyond a chimney and just barely there,
A sideways crescent moon. I tell you this
So you might come to the streets of Steubenville,
Springfield, and Detroit, and Gary, Indiana.

ON THE WAY

Someone had left a copy of the *Tao*,
A vase of cattails, and a writing pad
On the old motel dresser. Outside my room,
The traffic on Route 1 was constant
Far into the night. I wrote
To a full moon pale in the curtains
And a distant, barking dog. The next day
It rained as I drove. "Windex clean"
My parents would have called this morning,
Crows and seagulls in the air along the coast,
My destination *Weeping Gray*—your house
High as a hermit's cabin among the boulders.
You waited on the tiny lawn out back,
The painting before you only one stroke done,
Yet already in it, five tall misty flowers
Beside the empty pool and rainy path.

POEM FOR MY 44TH BIRTHDAY

I

More than midway through, I wake this morning
To the doctor's violin. He plays a Mozart sonata
And it's like a trembling wineglass spilling from its brim.
I lie a long while in bed, my thoughts
Upon Planck's Time, the splintered instant from which all life came
After that speck of space changed into matter, flung
Forth the universe. High on one wall
A sepia print in which a nude lies sprawled
Upon a Chinese robe. She, too, is composed, a physicist might say,
Of the matter of the stars, as all of us, all things
(The poplar leaf half-green, half-rot that sways
Outside my bedroom window) are composed. Then the music halts,
Leaving a little lap of silence in the air
Before the cicadas, a cardinal's two-note song,
The cars on the Merritt Parkway fill it in.

II

Late in the afternoon, my presents opened,
I backstroke Thrushwood Lake, watching for the muskrat
That lies in Boehmke's Cove. Twice each day
But not on schedule, he swims its length and back,
Leaving in his wake two intersecting V's.
The sky's the shade of blue that's almost white
(A Wedgewood color) and the twenty swaying willows
Seem great heads of hair from Merlin's world
Broken into ours. Turning, I remember
My daughter's love affair with miracles—how all
One afternoon when she was five she kept
Pointing at a rock, a tree, a flower, shouting

"Miracle! A miracle! A miracle!" until it sounded like
"America!" Walking the short way home,
I toss a pebble high into the air and catch it.

     III

After the evening television and the evening love,
I push the screen door open. It's a country night
Of lawn-chair shadows and the waning moon. Up in the field
Wings of bats and moths move silently
Like fragile waves of light and matter floating
Through all substances, or speckled images on photographic plates
Astronomers hold up: novas, quasars, pulsars flickered back in time.
If physicists are right, if I am not defined
By my form of body or my frame of mind
Am I set free to recognize and praise (the lovely obscure ways)
When consciousness aligns with harmonies? From next door
Mozart once again, this time on record, brief and dying,
And every house along my tiny street lies dark.
Down from the lake, a splash. Muskrat? Probably not.
Only a willow branch has fallen to the waters.

THE FLUTIST

My dreamy cousin, I see you standing on a ledge
Above the Batten Kill.
You seem to be waiting for someone,
Head to the side, your tall body all alert—

Even at sixteen
Already waiting, as if you already knew
The many small apartments, many small jobs
You would never quite want,

The men not quite loyal, the music
You love so much
Never quite perfected,
But blown from your lips the best that you knew how,

And your life, like most of ours,
A series of small recitals and arpeggios
Before a few
Ladies in folding chairs—

Waiting for someone, waiting
Almost on tiptoe
Upon a ledge, among the pines,
Above the Batten Kill.

CLIFF PAINTING

The girls who asked you to do it were the kind who leaned
Against you and no more. I don't think they knew the danger
Up there, at dawn when the cops wouldn't spot you.

I know I was scared. But I was also in love,
So deeply in love my hair would stand on end
Whenever I thought of her. That's why, one morning,

Brush and a can of paint in my old Boy Scout knapsack,
I started to climb. I was so crazy, I'd planned
To paint the biggest heart ever, and fill it with our names,

So the whole valley could see it, and every driver
On the Interstate—maybe even someone looking down
From a low-flying plane.... At first it was easy

As I passed the names of junior high school kids,
A few peace signs, a "Black is Beautiful," a "Stop the War,"
Several Bob Dylans and three Rolling Stones—

No pun intended. But then I began to come upon
The highest names, the ones from boys in college
On athletic scholarships, names of the weirdos

Who'd dare anything, and I realized I hadn't thought
This whole thing out enough. Every accessible place
Was taken with a name or heart, or both, and I knew

They must have used ropes, teams of boys with ropes
Had climbed before me, swinging out into space
To declare their love, allegiance, or obsession

At some risk of death.... I clung for a long time up there,
Looking down at the valley, thinking of my love, and hearing
What she would say if I failed. It started to drizzle

And a few small pebbles tumbled from the crevice
Where I was wedged. Pieces of moss came loose.
The valley darkened slightly. I closed my eyes and imagined

Falling, and my girl and parents at my funeral,
Then who she would marry instead.... And yet, you know,
I wanted fame and immortality right then—so if

Later I failed, wherever I was I could think of someone
Looking up at the cliff and seeing what I'd done, and maybe
For a moment I'd be someone other than a man

With a beer belly, sitting at a bar like this and reminiscing
Over what? Over love, that's what. I kept on climbing
And I found a place, I almost killed myself, but should

You look up now you'll see us, though the letters
Are somewhat faded and the heart looks like a kidney,
And later someone wrote above me even larger.

Still, I didn't marry her. At the end, we really fought
One night at the revival drive-in, Dean and Wood and Mineo
Together in the dark. She even wanted me

To climb again, to paint us over, and I laughed.
No way, I told her. Often I think of her trundling with her kids
And husband through the valley, and she glances

Up and there she is, with me again, forever
Linked with me upon the mountainside.... I'm glad I did it.
That's love for you. And also, that's revenge.

THE CLERGYMAN'S WIFE
COMPOSES A SPRING LETTER

His bad eye, the one that's losing vision,
Blurs, and much of the right side of his life
Becomes outline and vapor.
He's learning that he must turn consciously,
As toward a still life with a skull—the grapes
Overly ripe, shadows and moisture upon them,
And in those tiny caves where light has entered.

This evening, lurching to avoid the lights
Of a quickly approaching car, he stepped too far
Into wet blossoms of a fully blooming dogwood:
Incredible softness veined by deeper branches,
The momentary glowing as he groped for balance.
Reaching to catch him,
I saw the dried blood ending each white petal.

War was on TV when we returned, a blurry war
Waged by distant instruments and outright turnings,
And our children sat watching, their frozen bodies
Strewn upon the couch, the chairs, the rug.
It isn't pretty. It isn't the way I would have it,
But something is leaving us—the foliage behind it
Closing, as after a horseman riding through deep forest.

He's fine when it's dark and the room is very familiar,
Clock to the left of the dresser.
Our radio is playing us some Ives or Copland,
And he talks about the skyline of a county carnival,
A lighted ferris wheel revolving at its apex.
Love, he says, must have some swaying to it,
Some elevation and some desperateness.

Yet if only he could see whole! More and more often
He jerks his head sideways,

Sensing at his elbow what is nowhere near
Or only the padding of the cat across the floor.
His constant wandering is growing stronger,
As if he's finally understanding how we all
Must fumble in the grapevines for the skull.

Brave, blurry man. I love it when he touches
My face in the dark and asks me if I've seen
Angels or devils. I roll against him,
Not much to do, I know, but it is better
Than cursing or crying, punished past belief.
The irises came up, I meant to tell you,
And the heal-all on our lawn is one vast city.

THE PERFECT MIND

Each stone of the garden
Carefully set
After days of thought

So that anywhere
A leaf might fall
Will be correct.

BACKSTROKING AT THRUSHWOOD LAKE

Momentary beds of white burst flowers
    Appear behind us. Kicking and pulling,
We continually create what disappears,
    So keep from drowning.
And what a sky is overhead! Great medieval blurs
    Of cumulus ascending.

We reenact da Vinci's naked man
    With four arms, four legs, fingertips
And feet in square and circle to explain
    Proportion. Or imagine hips
Rocking in a snowfield: we have lain
    Down in snow, and left snow angel trails

From one side to the other, or a vertical
    String of paper dolls, joined head to toe across
Still waters. If we yell
    Out for the joy of it, or toss
Our heads from side to side, this spell
    Is exultation, just as it is madness.

Our elemental madness—that we know we live
    Today, this century, this year, this hour, minute
Everything is happening. Above,
    A flock of geese goes flying down towards Bridgeport.
Emerging in a high and cloudy cave,
    A Boeing's shadow is a crosslike print

To which you raise your head. The shore
    Is sand and willows—and our children
Floating near it, bobbing heads and figures
    Flattened on their plastic rafts. The wind
Blows them towards each other;
    Or away, unless they link their hands

While we tread water. Look at them. Their moments
　　Also disappear, yet last—the paradox
of memory. Think of mullein weeds,
　　Full and empty pods upon their stalks,
Dead flowers and the living seeds,
　　The washcloth texture of their flannel leaves,

And turn around. Stay close to me. Leave froth
　　Again behind us and to both our sides.
Nothing ever will be beautiful enough
　　Unless we're satisfied with how we ride
Waves backward and can love,
　　For what we fashion, though we cannot keep, we need—

As I, these living moments, need the lake against
　　My back, those towers in the clouds, the cries
Of children linking hands, the houses fenced
　　About the lake, their windows brimmed with sky
Blue and white—trapped in the way your glance
　　Catches me, and holds me, and all meanings fly.

BARGE LIGHTS ON THE HUDSON

for Dana and Mary Gioia

Glass door to the balcony slid open,
We step from the party to a night so clear
Only diamonds could scratch it. Below us,
River barges look like floating dominoes,
And we seem to hear boatmen singing, but that may
Be simply chanteys from another condominium
Along these cliffs. Hours, you say,
Should pass as slowly and as beautifully
As those lights on the Hudson. Leaning here
Against the railing, shoulders barely touching,
We play a child's game of connect-the-dots
To bring out of the dark a tiny tugboat
In which a phantom pilot, legs spread wide apart,
Wholeheartedly steers—his face
Rimose as the moon's. One by one,
Others join us, until all along
The balcony a line of men and women
Lean and whisper, staring down, and some
Say the river's asphalt, others that
U-galaxies drift there,
Or we are in a science-fiction movie
Watching starships in a planet exodus
Across the Coalsack. Soon, however,
The party flares up in the living room, those few
Who linger here grow silent, watching until all
Lights disappear toward Troy, and just the oars
Of Irving's ghost row out from Tarrytown.

END OF SPRING TERM

Although the clematis are out, it's still a somber morning
As we wait for our son. He should be crossing Pennsylvania now
In the dawn, the Greyhound bus tires steaming
Against the wet highway, and the residue
Of last tests still in his head. Perhaps he's just caught sight
Of a John Deere tractor climbing up a hill
Or one of those gray-wood houses you expect
To see in the distance when the mind's half full
Of sleep and thought. Or, head against his wadded sweater,
He's thinking of some girl. Or waterfall. I turn from the window
Where forty-four—I've counted—blossoms have appeared
Among the leaves that climb our trellised patio,
And try to be with him, remember everything
I can: voices over cards, the slight jouncing of a suitcase
In the overhead rack, tensed or untensed faces, the fling
Of bodies forward when the driver brakes in haste,
And boredom (boredom stays the same),
The towns, the villages brief flashings-by,
Birthdates, deathdates, lines and scenes and names,
All the facts and figures I once easily supplied
Fading into butter, buttercups, the rhododendron
And clematis by the porch, my parents on the lawn
They've left for me to cut. Not soon enough, but soon,
Philadelphia, and Newark, and New York, and home.

FINALE

The music was thrilling. But when we left the concert
Gullies of rain washed down between those buildings
Lining the dark street up to the subway station,
And pockmarked your naked shoulders as we walked
Slowly, resigned. For a moment, I thought
Of doing a bright Gene Kelly on the pavement,
But you looked so drowned, so unhappy
I bullied slightly ahead—the rainstorm too loud
Even for yelling. There is a tiny passage
In *Tender is the Night* where the hero, Dick Diver,
Knows everything's over. Everything. And it's so simple:
A brief streak of sky, a storefront boarded up,
Strands of wet hair plastering our skulls,
A thousand rainy windows to Far Rockaway.

Acknowledgments

▼

Grateful acknowledgment is given to the editors and publishers of the following, in which some of these new poems first appeared, a few in slightly changed versions:

The American Scholar ("Blanket Weather"), *The Atlantic Monthly* ("The Report"), *Boulevard* ("The New Transcendentalist," "Throwing Caution to the Winds"), *Chronicles* ("Parents Support Group"), *Crosscurrents* ("At Brown"), *The Gettysburg Review* ("M.F.A.," "Ode to the Cold War," "A Short History of the Vietnam War Years," "Three A.M."), *The Hudson Review* ("Letter from a Connecticut Country House," "On the New Haven Line," "Talking with Poets"), *Poetry* ("Another Knowledge," "The Narrow Mind," "The Same River, Twice," "Still Waters," "Time to Hear Ourselves Think"), *Urbanus* ("Cities of the Fifties"). "Talking with Poets" was reprinted in *The Best American Poetry: 1991*; "A Short History of the Vietnam War Years" was reprinted in *The Best American Poetry: 1994*.

The *Selected* poems were drawn from *Anon and Various Time Machine Poems* (Delacorte/Dell), *Regions With No Proper Names* (St. Martin's Press), *Overnight in the Guest House of the Mystic* (Louisiana State University Press), and *Flight and Pursuit* (Louisiana State University Press). Many of these poems first appeared in the following: *The Agni Review, The American Poetry Review, Bits, Contemporary Poets of New England, Connecticut River Review, Edge, Eleven, The Hudson Review, Michigan Quarterly Review, The Minnesota Review, Nassau Review, The New Criterion, The New Yorker, The North American Review, The Ontario Review, The Paris Review, Poetry, Poetry Miscellany, San José Studies, Silverfish Review, The Southern Review, Umbral, Western Humanities Review, The Wittenberg Review.*

My great thanks to the National Endowment for the Arts and the Ingram Merrill Foundation for poetry fellowships, which helped me to complete my previous books, and to the University of Bridgeport for granting me a sabbatical semester in 1996, which allowed me to complete this one.

Very special thanks to poets Cortney Davis, Frederick Feirstein, Dana Gioia, Sarah Gorham, Frederick Morgan, and Jeffrey Skinner.

The Author
▼

Dick Allen is a leading member of "the transition generation" of American poets who were born between the late 1930s and early 1940s. He was educated at Syracuse University and Brown University in the 1950s and 1960s. Currently, he is the Charles A. Dana Professor of English in the Humanities Department of the University of Bridgeport, where he is also Director of Creative Writing. Allen is the author or editor of nine previous books, including the National Book Critics Circle

Photo: Jon Gordon

Award Final Nominee, *Overnight in the Guest House of the Mystic* (Louisiana State University Press) and *Anon and Various Time Machine Poems* (Delacorte/Dell), *Regions With No Proper Names* (St. Martin's), *Flight and Pursuit* (Louisiana State University Press). He has received poetry writing fellowships from The National Endowment for the Arts and the Ingram Merrill Foundation, as well as Breadloaf's Robert Frost Poetry Fellowship, the Hart Crane Memorial Poetry Fellowship, *Poetry*'s Union Arts and Civic League Poetry Prize, the Poetry Society of America's Mary Caroline Davis Poetry Prize, and the San José Poetry Prize, among other honors. His individual poems have appeared in over one hundred of the nation's periodicals and anthologies, including *The American Poetry Review, The Antioch Review, The Atlantic Monthly, The Best American Poetry* volumes of 1991 and 1994, *Boulevard, Chicago*

Review, Contemporary Poetry in America, The Formalist, The Gettys-
burg Review, The Hudson Review, Image, The Michigan Quarterly
Review, The Modern Age, The New Criterion, The New Yorker, The
North American Review, The Ontario Review, The Paris Review,
Poetry, and *The Yale Review.* Dick Allen lives with his wife, fiction
writer Lori Negridge Allen, in a small cottage beside Thrushwood
Lake, in Trumbull, Connecticut. The Allens have two children,
music critic Rev. Richard Negridge Allen and poet Tanya Angell
Allen.